Modernize Your Law Firm

Modernize Your Law Firm

Transform Your Law Firm for the Future

Lynda Artesani

BUSINESS EXPERT PRESS

Leader in applied, concise business books

Modernize Your Law Firm: Transform Your Law Firm for the Future

Copyright © Business Expert Press, LLC, 2024

Cover design by M Mjajid from Hasnain Coverz

Interior design by Exeter Premedia Services Private Ltd., Chennai, India

First published in 2023 by
Business Expert Press, LLC
222 East 46th Street, New York, NY 10017
www.businessexpertpress.com

ISBN-13: 978-1-63742-559-6 (paperback)
ISBN-13: 978-1-63742-560-2 (e-book)

Business Expert Press Business Law and Corporate Risk Management Collection

First edition: 2023

10 9 8 7 6 5 4 3 2 1

I have a few very important people in my life that I would like to acknowledge and dedicate this book.

To my loving husband, Michael Artesani.

Your unwavering support and belief in my dreams have been the foundation of my journey. Your encouragement, patience, and understanding have given me the strength to pursue my passions and embrace new challenges. This book is a testament to our shared commitment to each other and the boundless possibilities we create together. Thank you for being my rock and for always standing by my side. This achievement is as much yours as it is mine.

To my incredible business partner, Sarah Prevost.

Working alongside you has been a true privilege. Your exceptional dedication, sharp insights, and steadfast commitment to excellence have shaped our accounting firm. Together, we have overcome hurdles, celebrated victories, and embraced the power of innovation. Your unwavering belief in our shared vision has driven us to new heights. This book is dedicated to you, Sarah, for being the best business partner one could ask for. Here's to our continued success and many more remarkable ventures together.

And to my dear friend, Marianne Holmes.

Throughout the writing of this book, you have been my guiding star. Your unyielding support, thoughtful feedback, and creative inspiration have been invaluable. Your accomplishments as a fiction writer have continually inspired me to push the boundaries of my creativity. Your friendship has filled this journey with motivation and profound growth. Thank you, Marianne, for challenging, believing in me. This book is dedicated to you as a symbol of our enduring friendship and shared passion for the written word.

With each of you, your love, support, and unwavering belief in me have transformed my dreams into reality. May this book stand as a tribute to our unbreakable bonds and a testament to the incredible power of collaboration, friendship, and unwavering support.

Description

Unlocking Success in the Digital Age: Transform Your Law Firm for the Future.

In today's rapidly evolving digital age, it's become crucial for law firms to modernize and adapt to stay ahead of the competition. With advancements in technology and a shift in client expectations, it's essential for law firms to embrace digital transformation to remain relevant and successful. But where should you start? In this book, I outline essential steps that your law firm needs to take to modernize and thrive in the digital age.

From leveraging digital billing solutions to integrating cloud-based practice management software, we'll provide actionable tips and insights to help you streamline your operations, enhance client satisfaction, and increase your firm's overall efficiency and profitability. By implementing these steps, you'll not only position your law firm as a forward-thinking and innovative practice but also be able to attract and retain a larger client base.

Don't get left behind in this digital revolution—join me as I guide you through the process of modernizing your law firm and show you how to stay ahead in the fast-paced digital age.

Keywords

law firm modernization; digital transformation for law firms; legal tech advancements; digital marketing strategies for lawyers; cloud-based practice management software; streamlining law firm operations; enhancing client satisfaction in legal practice; increasing law firm efficiency; improving law firm profitability; innovative legal practices; adapting to the digital age in the legal field; staying ahead in the legal industry; attracting and retaining legal clients; law firm digital revolution; forward-thinking legal practices

Contents

Testimonials

"Lynda Artesani crafted a fantastic resource with so much depth and knowledge on the history of accounting for law firms. From the historical to today, I appreciate your stories, tips, and ideas on moving from passe to a robust and efficient law firm!"—**Sarah Prevost, Mintage Labs | The Proper Trust LLC, Founder/Cofounder**

"Lynda Artesani has produced the first book I have ever read on law firms and how they operate, which makes total sense. This is from the perspective of operations and accounting, which is so often overlooked within the legal industry. It is often taken for granted that the accounting and operations functions will somehow take care of themselves, usually with less desirable results.

In this book, Lynda takes us on a thought-provoking journey through the myriad of subjects the Modern Law Firm needs to consider to be on the cutting edge of technology, systems, operations, and ultimately, success with their business. She has the experience and the 'know-how' to patiently lead the reader through what it takes to modernize their law firm sensibly and creatively for improvement by following her historical analysis of systems and how they have changed today ... for the better."—**Steve Libhart, Numbers Matter, LLC, Founder**

"Lynda Artesani's book Modernize Your Law Firm *provides invaluable insights into the key performance indicators and best practices for law firm operations. Her approach to centralizing law firm accounting in a professional and trusted platform and automating workflows with open-source technology is a game-changer for firms looking to streamline their operations. Her expertise in finding the right legal tech software is unparalleled. As a legal tech CEO, I encourage you to heed her wisdom and learnings when building the operational functions of your law firm! Her book is a must-read for law firm owners and managers looking to run more profitable and efficient businesses."*—**Jonathan Fishman, LeanLaw, CEO and Founder**

CHAPTER 1

History of Law Firm Workflows

Predigital Days

Technology has made it much simpler and easier to perform routine tasks that law firms typically need to get done. The legal field isn't the same as a short decade ago, back when they had to rely on copies of physical contracts and paper catalogs of online research databases. These advancements have made life easier for lawyers, not to mention their clients!

When we look back at technology pre-1980s, the law firm had dictation machines, a typewriter, telephones, maybe a Paymaster check writer, and a calculator. That was our technology in the predigital days. I still remember seeing the first fax machine coming into an office and being amazed that the fax machine sent a document somehow through a phone line. How did it do that?

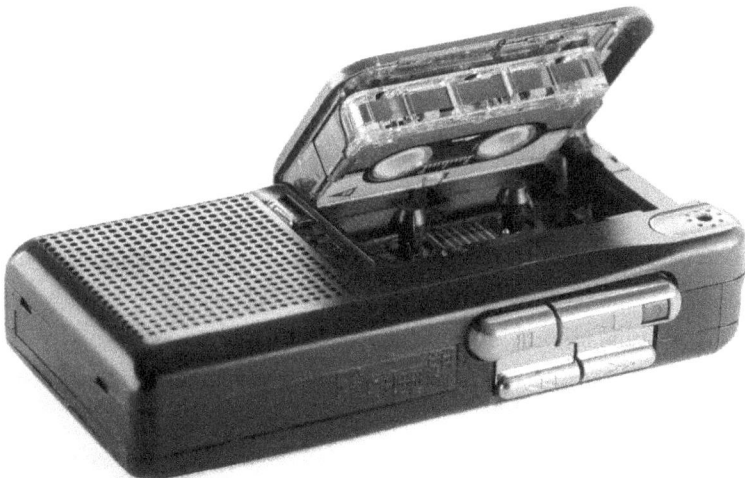

How did we speed up processes in the predigital days? Well, we relied on memorization and the human brain. Remember shorthand? It was an effective way for an attorney to dictate to the assistant or secretary. That secretary would then produce a document for the case to the client. That was the extent of our "technology" to save time effectively.

The dictation machine was first introduced to law firms in the mid-1950s. It was a machine that freed up schedules and saved time. No longer did an attorney need to be present to dictate to their assistant. They could record the language they wanted to be put in a document, and their assistant could use it to type up the legal documents at another time.

And what about research? Attorneys performed their research by poring through law book after law book to research an article, a case, or research laws. This method was very time-consuming and cumbersome. Conducting legal research was difficult before the era of digital databases. One had to rely solely on hard copies and books for such a task and hopefully the right hard copy or law book.

Before we move on to what changed to improve all of this, let's consider change itself. Anyone who has ever worked with others in an office setting probably knows how difficult it is to change how work is performed. There is resistance to anything that isn't "The Way We Do It." Conversations go this way:

"Have you ever tried doing x?"
"No, that's not The Way We Do It."
Or, maybe:
"I think it might be easier if we try x."
"That's not The Way We Do It."

The first challenge is getting buy-in for new systems, equipment, software, timeframes—anything that changes how work is done. Why? Because people are threatened by change. Will this make me/my job obsolete? What if I can't learn the new way? What if it doesn't work? We're doing the job; why change something that's working now?

We tend to fall back on what we already know—The Way We Do It.

Despite the emotions, we can probably agree that some change is necessary. Much change is beneficial. Some change fosters growth and

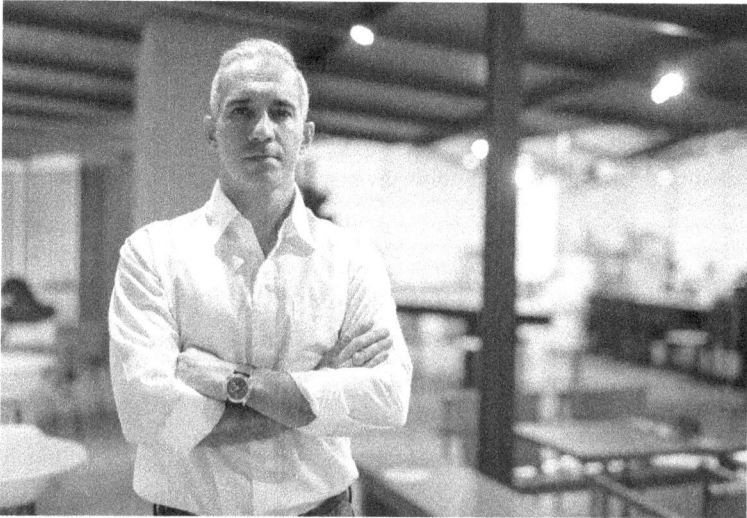

better working conditions. Automating your practice is about all these characteristics of evolution. A robust and positive attitude approaching new business methods starts at the top. Being open-minded, setting an example of acceptance, and being willing to learn new ways of doing things will go a long way in helping staff do the same. Be the technology champion for your firm!

How PCs Changed the Legal Industry

Legal Research

In the not-too-distant past, research was generally a long drawn out and tedious endeavor. Attorneys had to pore through stacks of books and documents from libraries, both private and public, and then cling to little slips of paper with markings that were made as they researched case law. However, there was no guarantee that every single piece of information ever published was found or made available to them during their process of legal research. During this time, the only real search engine they had was the human brain and while this is indeed wonderful when it comes to storage and recall capabilities, it still has its limits when it comes time for storage.

With their library of legal records, attorneys and legal professionals can more easily find relevant documents, case-law decisions, and research materials for given cases. Enter the personal computer and computerized records and attorneys can quickly search and sort by date or by name, making document retrieval about as easy as clicking a link for a more organized process of pulling and copying pertinent resources.

When it comes down to legal research, a good lawyer wants to make sure that they are going to be thorough and find all the details that might fill in gaps between the spaces here and there. It's just like running an advanced search on Google—you need powerful computer programs specializing in law like Westlaw and Lexis Nexis, which allow users to run particularly intricate searches for compelling cases that are extremely case-dependent.

Because courts rely on case law to make decisions about a particular topic, an attorney must have legal precedents and lines of applicable case-law opinions demonstrating the universal soundness of their position. An attorney who lacks these tools will have great difficulty making legal arguments because they can't draft convincing motions, win appeals, or even understand the issue at hand. But if they present them very clearly in front of the judge, then they will set themselves up for success.

Analyzing Briefs

Today, new lawyers use digital technology extensively. But it was not that many years back that analyzing briefs was a very manual process. A good legal brief contains a lot of details. Our electronic products could never replace the written process completely.

As in so many other areas, when analyzing briefs, isn't the human brain required? There is no way a computer could mimic what is necessary to do this work, right? Well, enter IBM's Watson and cognitive learning and artificial intelligence (AI).

Watson, an artificially intelligent computer system capable of answering questions posed in natural language, was developed in IBM's DeepQA project between 2001 and 2004. In 2011, Watson competed on the U.S. game show Jeopardy against former champions Brad Rutter and Ken Jennings. In a three-game match, Watson won $1 million by beating them both. The system is capable of understanding questions posed in natural language and responding with statistically driven hypotheses expressed as affirmative or negative sentences.

If you watched Watson compete with the Jeopardy players, some of its answers were perfectly articulated but some were quite comical. AI cannot quite replace the human brain; however, it wields some amazing ability to assist attorneys in the analysis of far more data more quickly than anything ever has in the past.

Bookkeeping/Accounting

I have seen the evolution of bookkeeping firsthand. I remember my accounting classes in high school where we had to use huge green grid sheets to keep track of our expenses. We had to add up the columns with a pencil and make sure we had a good eraser so we could erase any mistakes. Nowadays, bookkeeping is done digitally and it's so much easier to keep track of everything.

The next innovation that appeared was One-Write Plus. It was a bookkeeping program that was still paper-centric. But it was like a giant book that had carbon paper. You had copies of all the checks. It also came in a format in which you could put the expenses in a column to create the profit and loss.

My first experiences doing accounting with the One-Write Plus program were quickly followed by the entry of computers. Personal computers on desks had programs that could be used to aggregate the data in a better way. The next step came when QuickBooks, the accounting platform, was introduced, and I've continued to use that product since 1999.

Studying the output from an organized analysis of data from a platform like QuickBooks was a significant shift in tracking and studying bookkeeping. All this keyboard entry did indeed save time compared to handwriting all the transactions for a business.

Looking back, I find it incredible how far technology has progressed.

Tracking Accounts Receivable

I've been doing bookkeeping and accounting work for over 20 years now. I like to use the term "back in my day" in reference to when I started doing my bookkeeping work; it was a manual and prolonged process.

For example, processing was very paper-centric. In the old days of law firm billing, it was done by creating invoices on a typewriter on letterhead, maybe with carbon paper. Once personal computers (PCs) were introduced, we did the Accounts Receivable by typing something into a Microsoft Word document.

It was very segmented and full of duplicated tasks.

Once the invoice was typed, the next logical step was for it to be entered into the accounting software. As you can imagine, there is redundancy in this workflow. The multiple steps in this process, often involving several different individuals, thereby increased the likelihood of errors.

As technology progressed, I can still fondly remember the day when we could create an invoice within the accounting software using QuickBooks Desktop. It was exciting to see that we could make two steps, or even multiple steps, become one.

In the early days of using QuickBooks Desktop, we were still in the pre-e-mail days. We entered invoices and printed the invoices, and then mailed them. I still run into law firms printing and sending these documents by snail mail. Knowing the tools that are now available, I find this workflow so unnecessarily slow and manual.

Now, when did this process break down? Quite simply, where any workflow will break down with manual processes. Even in today's world, where attorneys are still using desktop products, we see disjointedness because the legal software is separate from the accounting software.

For example, you create an invoice out of Microsoft Word or the TimeSlips desktop product, but you forget to enter it into the accounting software. This error usually gets caught when a client pays you, and you notice that the entry for the invoice didn't happen. But what happens if they don't pay you? Or pay something other than the invoiced amount?

I've also seen firms that use external software or even a Microsoft Word type of product, and then they don't enter the income in an individualized format. They use a journal entry to book in any monies received as legal services income and bypass the entire Accounts Receivable workflow. I've often seen a client create an invoice, enter a client payment, and deposit it to an undeposited funds account in QuickBooks. Then they will either create a journal entry for income based on the total deposits from their bank statement or enter the bank feed and download it as direct income. This process results in a duplication of the income on the books.

No one wants to be taxed twice on the same income.

Accounts Receivable tracking was not easy in the predigital days. Accounts Receivable was entirely manual before accounting software was a part of a law firm's daily work processes. Most likely, it was monitored on a piece of paper or typed in some manner where you tracked open invoices and paid invoices.

In the early days, that software may have been a spreadsheet called "Lotus 1-2-3." Does anyone remember that? I can remember creating large spreadsheets, and then if I clicked to exit the program, there was nothing there to remind me to hit "save" first. I would lose all the information and must recreate it. It made me want to cry!

As you can see from what I've outlined previously, all the segmented workflows can take much time to process and can lead to missing data. No one ever wants to find that an invoice was forgotten, or payments weren't tracked. And you can't afford to neglect to follow up with a client who has not paid.

Tracking Accounts Payable

When I think back to the processes, we used for Accounts Payable in the predigital days, all I can think about is the paper. Does anyone really like to file?

Many moons ago, we would receive the bills via the U.S. Postal Service at the office. They may have been opened by a file clerk and placed on my desk. I remember the time it took to sort by the vendor or supplier and stack up the individual items.

Next, we would enter the bills into the accounting software. The "software" in this case was that big, old-fashioned checkbook-style binder in my early days as a bookkeeper. You would write all the details into the book, pressing hard with your pen to penetrate through the layers of carbon paper.

I remember having that desk drawer where I had my filing system, which was an expandable folder. As I entered the bills for the week, I would place the processed bills into this expandable folder with the alphabet letters on the tabs, filing each vendor bill under the first initial of the company name.

On Friday, I would pay the bills by pulling them out of the expandable folder, going through them, and selecting the ones to be paid that week. That's when I would use the "Paid" stamp, carefully enter the check number, and file it away in the vendor's manila folder.

I would manually calculate or even tally up the total vendor payments on a calculator. Then I would write the check, using that check writer machine, which would impress into the check stock to add the total vendor payment amount officially.

Are we done here? Of course not. Next, I would stamp the bills from my vendors, and code them to an expense category by writing the code in the box, and then I would use the "entered" stamp to mark it as entered. Once I paid a vendor, I would use a "paid" stamp and staple all the bills together. And then I would still have to file it all.

Efficient? Not at all. In those days, a full-time job existed around handling these details that today would just take hours.

After thinking back to this past workflow, I am so glad I live and work in current times. Automating this process in a much better way allows me more time to do the things that I feel are more important for my clients.

Client Contact

In the predigital days, most clients chose their attorneys by word of mouth or by searching for them on the Yellow Pages. In those early days, when a new client signed up at the law firm, it was handled by typing in a customer card that would go in a standing file, almost like a Rolodex. The standing file would hold the important information on the client, such as name and address, phone number, matter name, maybe a client ID or matter number.

Additionally, once a client became a customer of the firm, the office staff would create a file folder and file it away in the big old gray filing cabinet.

This work was often handled by a receptionist and in the very early days of predigital, it was done by the law clerk.

Fast forward to a time when we began to see some computers arriving on desks. We used to use a program called "Access" by Microsoft.

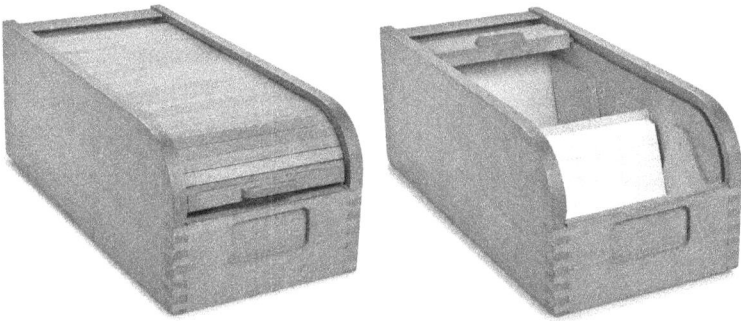

The program was state of the art. Instead of keeping everything on a sheet of paper, you were able to manage your contacts quite simply. Having this ability to aggregate and sort through the contacts made it easier to market the law firm.

Processing/Analyzing Client Information

Processing and analyzing client data required significant human resources before computer assistance was available. The human brain had to comb through details that a simple computer search would quickly and efficiently handle today. The opportunities for errors and omissions were much greater.

This was, again, a paper-intensive process, with valuable hours being devoted to shuffling and reading documents. Documents could be lost or misplaced as they were handled by multiple people.

And, of course, all of this was subject to human interpretation, making it difficult to achieve consistency.

Scheduling/Tracking Billable Hours

Tracking billable hours and scheduling was typically done by the secretary or legal assistant. In the early days, we did this manually. I can still remember the paper calendars; you could write your appointments on them. I also remember when electronic calendars appeared in the modern office, and when I suggested using one, my boss didn't want to give up his paper calendar. These calendars were enormous and took up the entire desktop. The large space allowed the user to write appointments in each block for each day.

You could write the start time of the meeting or the start time that you began working on a case or matter, and then you'd write the end time. It was up to the person doing the bookkeeping to do the calculation of billable time and then do the invoicing. The attorney would tear off the sheet and hand it to the billing person. A job like this could fill your day.

It's interesting that in the 1800s, the billable hours were capped by state law. Restricting billable hours put a "cap" on how much a law firm could successfully generate as legal income from legal services. Back then, the losing party paid for any matter that was litigated.

It wasn't until the 1930s and 1940s that the legal industry changed dramatically. No longer were billable hours capped by state law. The state bar associations began publishing minimum fees per case or matter and would fine firms that billed below those minimums. The American Bar Association (ABA) model code stayed in effect until 1969 when it "deemed it unethical to undercharge."

The most comical part of this historical path that legal billing took for law firms is that the shift started because attorneys were upset that the dentists were out earning them. I always like to say that a good attorney is competitive (www.lawpeopleblog.com/2007/06/a-short-history-of-the-billable-hour-and-the-consequences-of-its-tyranny/).

I used this article as a reference and want to give the writer credit.

Marketing Services

Today, I think we rely more on Google and Google reviews as a referral source to find an attorney. But years ago, before Google, this industry relied heavily on word-of-mouth.

So the client experience was significant in the early days because a happy client would refer you. And, an unhappy client could damage your reputation. These facts continue to be factors today, but marketing has changed in other ways. For example, the speed of information, good or bad, makes it nearly impossible to control the damage. And social media provides many, and sometimes inexpensive, means of advertising.

The other marketing method in the past was the Yellow Pages. And, boy, was it expensive. In those days of marketing your law firm, the Yellow Pages salesman would come into your office randomly and unannounced. And then the hard sell would begin. Did you want to be that fancy law firm with the big shiny ad? And, if you wanted to change your mind and your ad, you had to wait until the next publication, typically a year later.

Today, as in the past, you need to know if your marketing is effective. You need to track the foot traffic or phone calls or whatever means a client uses to reach out to your firm. Technology offers tools to easily track those metrics in whatever degree of detail you need.

Business Key Performance Indicators

Ever since there have been methods of tracking your bookkeeping, even written methods, there has been a need to track key performance indicators (KPIs). It is imperative to know the metrics at your law firm, as well as how to tweak them to make improvements. My favorites include profitability by case or matter, utilization rate, realization rate, and marketing. Historically, this was done on a separate grid sheet or spreadsheet. The difficulty here is that it was a time-intensive process. Tracking KPIs came more into vogue with the ability to sort through data when computers were introduced to law firms.

Attorney Productivity/Efficiency

Attorney productivity is always essential to know; the future of the firm depends on the attorneys at the firm doing profitable work. Although we'd like to think that an attorney works eight hours per day on billable work, that's not always the case. There's lunch and a coffee break, sometimes there's training required to keep their licenses to practice law or stay current in their specialties. When examining how many hours per day an attorney works versus the number of hours billed out, you are determining your utilization rate.

Productivity is something that mid-market firms are nearly always looking to change. Many clients have asked us to create benchmarks around these essential metrics to see how well an attorney is doing.

Are they pulling their weight? Are they bringing in the revenue? Now you can get a little more complex when you track the realization rate or look at how many hours billed were collected and paid. That can change the formula results dramatically.

Most Profitable Clients/Cases/Areas

Just as it is important to measure attorney productivity, knowing which cases or matters are profitable is key to running a successful office. Maybe your firm has multiple practice areas. Which area is bringing in the most money per matter? Of course, in the precomputer days, we did this manually and relied heavily on instinct. You would tally up the hours the attorneys worked and do the math quite simply. Not a particularly efficient way to do it, but it yields the estimated results that a practicing attorney or partner needs to know when managing a law firm.

The math is simple:

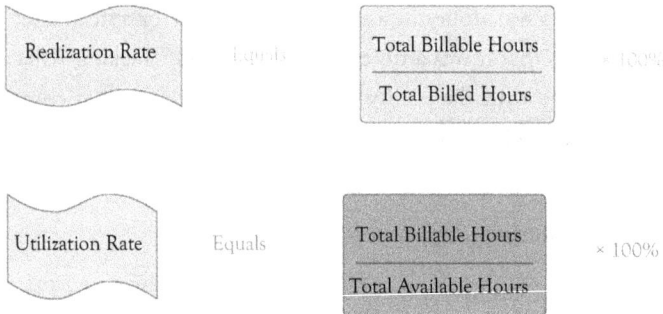

$$\text{Realization Rate} \quad \text{Equals} \quad \frac{\text{Total Billable Hours}}{\text{Total Billed Hours}} \times 100\%$$

$$\text{Utilization Rate} \quad \text{Equals} \quad \frac{\text{Total Billable Hours}}{\text{Total Available Hours}} \times 100\%$$

Source: This picture was created by Lynda Artesani.

Centralized Platform Needed

A successful law firm needs an open platform that connects to the financial institutions that it interacts with, where it can find support anywhere, anytime, from any device. You want to put your firm's accounting into a tool that you trust as there is nothing more important than safeguarding your financial information. Having your firm's accounting software on a server is very expensive and pretty much a thing of the past. It does not keep your data more secure.

For a law firm, when we talk about a "centralized platform," we are talking about a customer relationship management (CRM) tool.

The sticking point tends to be inertia. Ask your team if they like their time tracking software. Does it serve their needs? Everyone wants the results produced by change, but no one looks forward to living through it. Plan on it taking 90 days to institutionalize good software.

But, once you get there, you are opening yourself and your firm up to new possibilities. Having your law firm accounting in professional hands will save you both money and time. You can take more time off. You can do pro bono work. You can spend time with your family. You will have a more compliant practice.

Ensure Good Communication Within the Firm

Some of the best CRM programs are the ones that help a law firm manage their leads from the start or initial call to becoming a client to finishing the matter. You never want to miss a lead or not follow up with one. These systems work by setting up repetitive tasks and will remind you when it's time to follow up. You can customize them to work for your practice area.

Many apps sync accounting with timekeeping and invoicing. The sync should happen seamlessly behind the scenes. And it should be automatic. Some of the legal software doesn't sync with the accounting software at all or has to be manually pushed.

There are pluses and minuses to both software types. Typically, with that all-in-one software, you lose out on some technology from an add-on software because everything is baked into one software, and you cannot layer other tools onto it.

That is why my preference is to start with a robust accounting system, one that allows you to create an automated workflow that is open source. Having that sync-type application layered with the accounting opens many doors. Add the legal tech and the robust system just becomes legal industry specific.

Finding the Right Legal Tech Software

Imagine software that looks like this:

You collect your time and track it by matter, either via the Web login or your phone, while you're in court. Client expenses are managed and imported using an outside software in which you can easily precode and push the data along with a copy of the expense attached to the line item within the accounting software. As the month closes, your admin or bookkeeper pushes the legal time tracked and expenses into a draft bill. You review the bill, and make any adjustments, like writing down billable hours, removing billable hours and saving them for the next billing moment, or any adjustments on expenses. Next, with one click, you move all of that into the approved sections of the bookkeeper or admin. Then, once again with one click, move the data as an invoice to your client and add it to the accounting. Does that sound like a dream? This technology exists today. No more paper and no more missed expenses. Let's face it—your staff is really busy, and this is when errors tend to occur. The combination of software makes slight work of managing billing your clients.

With larger firms, there is a need for user permission levels in areas such as accounts receivable and client management. Perhaps you need an arrangement in which several admins need access to the slightly different areas of accounts receivable for which they are responsible. With the right tools in the right hands, your office can be selective, efficient, and secure.

Ensure Good Communication Between Firm and Clients

Some firms generate a massive volume of invoices each month, with varied terms and methods of payment. You would need at least one full-time employee to manage that workflow. Do you need the ability to mass produce many templated invoices for many clients in less time and with less effort?

The more quickly an invoice is received, the more quickly it can be paid. Increased cash flow from timely payments gives law firms the freedom to make more expansive operational decisions.

Overloaded Staff and Costly Mistakes

Whether you are working with completely remote staff or a hybrid arrangement, the software helps with communication among attorneys, legal assistants, and paralegals. No more waiting to get answers and approvals.

Some of the best parts of the CRM software allow for segments to be automated and maintain the client relationship. We all get very busy in our work, and this means no steps are missed and no deadlines are missed. Some of the best software includes a timeline for the case or matter and the firm can set up the steps that work best and finesse them as necessary.

The right platform can save your firm significant time, as well as money, through efficiencies. You can bring in data from your bank, and from case or practice management software. This eliminates the need for double entry, and means less time spent searching for errors. You can use automation tools to send out invoices with payment links for ease of collecting. You can create specialized reports and import data. With the manual drudgery of reconciliation solved by automation, you can focus your efforts on more elevated tasks.

This is not the software to skimp on. A great CRM will provide great results.

Enable All to Focus on Work

How hard are you working to get your data? Do you need to ask someone else to get it for you? Is there a lot of manual work involved? Why not switch to something more modern and, ultimately, less expensive?

Automation of this nature allows attorneys, associates, and paralegals to work on the same file and do their respective jobs. This will help with any redundancy in the workflow and any missed steps will be apparent within the timeline.

If your firm is growing, you want the ability to take a snapshot of the fiscal health of your operation—daily, weekly, monthly. The right reports will help you focus on forecasting, budgeting, improving cash flow, and using your knowledge to become more prosperous.

When you have your financial operations automated, along with the consultation of a true law accounting expert, you will have freed up your time and your employees' time to work on more valued tasks. For you, to focus on your casework. For your employees, to be reassigned to new, higher level tasks that return more value to the firm.

Notifications for Approval and Timely Reminders

The technology is such that repetitive tasks can be automatically performed repeatedly. Many of the hard deadlines are the same for each type of case or matter. Automation means that nothing is missed in the workflow, especially when several members of the team are working on the same matter.

It's a seamless way to do the work and not have to worry about coding the deadlines in a calendar. That's done for you. Templates can be well-defined, created, and used specifically for your firm. When a task is completed, you can set the system up to notify everyone that the work is done and it's time to move on to the next step.

The New Environment: Permanent Changes to Law Firm Operations

Why the New Environment?

There is a new environment brewing in the legal industry. And that new environment is not the standard downtown law office full of employee cubicles and fancy corner offices.

We are starting to see a unique scenario, almost a perfect storm. We see attorneys from different places around the country working remotely from home. Their entire support staff is virtual. When there's a need for a conference room, one is just rented. These partnerships are formed, and a partnership agreement is in place. The beauty of this model is that there is much flexibility around the staff. We are starting to see the traditional law firm model morph into this hybrid model. There may be an office rented, but it's small, and paralegals and other supporting staff work from home.

Working from home may sound like utopia, and it can be an excellent situation for young parents, but this model has some barriers. Innovation and collaboration can be lost when people aren't in the same room together, brainstorming ideas and methodology. I believe that some of the best insights are formulated at that conference room table in the law office. Additionally, with the traditional model, younger lawyers learn from their older, more seasoned peers.

Hence, a firm may opt for an office with the traditional model, but there's no reason they can't adopt great technology. Automation can be implemented with software and a finely tuned workflow for your firm. Finessing the setup does take a bit of time to accomplish, but it's worth it in the long run. Automation equals nearly perfect data. Nothing is ever overlooked.

COVID Requirements

The shift in some law firms to a more hybrid style was triggered by the pandemic. With COVID as a factor, law firm staff were forced to work from their homes. It was an easy transition for some firms that had already moved to cloud-based technology.

For the firms still living with servers and desktop software, an urgent move to work from home was not as simple. Not only was there an immediate shift to move the firm to become cloud-based, but a barrier arose in the form of training staff in the new software. Now they had to train on the software remotely. Not ideal. The learning curve is steep.

I am reminded of one law firm that we were working with just before the onset of the pandemic. We were moving them over to a cloud-based workflow. This firm was very paper-centric and was using an antiquated desktop program. They had not ever used Zoom before they engaged with our firm. None of the firm's staff had cameras or microphones on their computers.

They quickly adapted to Zoom and loved the meetings in which we trained in the new software. The firm soon ordered Logitech cameras for their PCs, and within a month of our training, the United States was in full lockdown mode. Seriously scary times.

This law firm adapted to Zoom quickly, and we had so much fun with the backgrounds and some of the Zoom features, including some silly characters and the fake makeup, which was still a Beta feature in Zoom. You can imagine the laughter around fake computer-generated eyebrows and lips hanging in space. It helped relieve a little of the tension and drama surrounding the time we live in. It was nice to be able to use technology as a welcome distraction.

Changes Adopted as a Result of COVID

There have been fundamental changes post COVID. Many times, it's the younger person at the law firm who drives the changes and implements new technology. Millennial or Gen Z attorneys and staff members may implement more modern technology and all it takes is others in the office to see the ease of automation. Even reluctant staff members are drawn to the processes, which mean that they don't have to type data manually anymore. Most repeatable tasks can be automated with good technology. Generally, with a couple of clicks the data is entered. For example, using text expander software allows you to use shortcuts. Imagine how much time you can save when writing a legal draft.

Sometimes I work with firms in which some of the parties are reluctant to change. Maybe it's just one person who is not on board with a shift. We explain that technology is not going to replace the human mind, it's going to assist in enhancing your ability to do your work. Even the most seasoned partner in a firm has used the technology on their phone. Typically, that analogy is my first avenue to open their minds to change. It allows us to have that first conversation regarding using transactional technology at the workplace.

I genuinely believe that COVID was that kick in the rear that some lawyers needed to begin to adopt change. We got rid of that old "if it's not broke, don't fix it" mentality. There's some good data and science behind the fact that the brain doesn't want to change what we know, especially when we are very comfortable with what we know. But there's even better science behind learning new technologies and growing more neurons, sparking the brain, and creating new pathways. Not to mention the efficiencies we can create in the workplace!

Another example of someone not wanting to embrace change happened when we worked with a law firm in which the admin was so comfortable with an old desktop program that she refused to stop working on it. She used both the new system and the old system. She did double the work. This repetitive workflow wasn't discovered for months. She was so at ease with the old software that she didn't want to let it go. It wasn't until we asked her for a report that we discovered what she was doing.

To convince her to let go of the old software, we did a test of two similar tasks, one in the old software and one in the new. As she clicked away, we counted the clicks. One, two, three, finally she reached eleven. Then we shifted to the cloud-based system and entered the same data. One deposit, three clicks. We convinced her!

Other Factors

Besides COVID, there are other factors driving the legal industry to adopt new technology. I can think of one particularly timely example. In today's world of the Great Recession and the driving up of wages, why not automate the heck out of your workflow? Technology is galloping along and if you don't hop on the train, you will fall behind your colleagues and peers. Adopting cloud technology will not only improve the accuracy of the work but enable you to produce more work with fewer people and it can be done rather quickly and efficiently.

AI still seems like a futuristic dream. In today's world of processing transactions, you can look to programs that see patterns and start to develop "suggestions." Just look at Google mail. As you type an e-mail to a client, Google suggests the words for you and makes writing or drafting an e-mail quicker and easier than ever. I expect to see this process get better, more efficient, and speedier. We see this within QuickBooks in the bank feeds. Just a few short years ago, bank feeds were interesting and time saving. But the suggestions there were not great. Today, you can use rules and the suggestions to move quickly through 1,000 or so transactions that a year ago would have taken the bookkeeper a full two to three days to input.

ChatGPT

This is certainly a buzz word at the time of writing this book. And for those of us who love technology, it is exciting. I have had some colleagues play with this new AI-generated software and the results, when prompting the software properly, are incredible. I opened ChatGPT and asked a few questions:

what is law droid

Lawdroid is a term used to refer to a legal technology platform that uses artificial intelligence and machine learning to automate various legal tasks. This technology is designed to help lawyers and legal professionals streamline their workflows, reduce manual effort, and improve accuracy. Some common applications of Lawdroid technology include legal research, contract review and analysis, document generation, and e-discovery. The goal of Lawdroid is to enhance the efficiency and effectiveness of legal work by reducing the time and effort required to perform routine or repetitive tasks, freeing up lawyers to focus on more strategic and high-value activities. However, it is important to note that Lawdroid technology does not replace the expertise of human lawyers and is typically used as an assistive tool.

what is chatgpt

ChatGPT is an open-source language model developed by OpenAI, a research organization focused on advancing artificial intelligence. It is a conversational AI model that has been trained on a large corpus of text from the internet and has the ability to generate human-like responses to natural language text inputs. ChatGPT is designed to support various applications, including chatbots, question-answering, and content generation. It uses a transformer architecture, which is a deep learning model that has achieved state-of-the-art performance on several natural language processing tasks. ChatGPT can be used to generate text outputs for various purposes, such as generating product descriptions, composing articles, or answering questions.

It literally answered these two questions in seconds! I see this is the next big "thing" that will revolutionize the accounting world and the legal world too. For attorneys, the excitement comes in the form of Lawdroid.

This will revolutionize legal research. Much like ChatGPT, this AI learns as it develops. If you want to be that cutting-edge attorney, sign up for Lawdroid and be an early adopter.

Blockchain

Blockchain has always fascinated this self-described numbers-geek. With Blockchain technology, we can store information in a transparent fixed ledger. When we think of blockchain, automatically our brains go to bitcoin. But law firms can use blockchain for transactional legal services and smart contracts with the terms of the agreement directly written into code. Think of how amazing this would be for Contract Law or Real Estate law practice areas!

Or imagine using blockchain for evidence management. Blockchain can be used to store and manage evidence in a secure, tamper-proof manner, which can improve the efficiency and transparency of legal proceedings.

This use of technology would be a game-changer and will all but eliminate transactional errors.

Cybercrime

Cyberattacks are becoming increasingly sophisticated. They're often carried out by people trying to steal money or information. Even the ABA has cited this as an "urgent concern" for law firms. As per the ABA, 25 percent of law firms have experienced a data breach. That's a lot of law firms.

Does your law firm use a Wi-Fi system that is shared with staff and clients? Is there a guest Wi-Fi login and password? Who at the firm is aware of the password for the business Wi-Fi? This information should be documented.

Document all the software that's used at the law firm. Who has the master or primary admin seat? It should always be held by a partner or someone responsible for the accounting data at the law firm. It should not be an admin or a legal secretary. It should be the owner of the firm.

Who has access to the software? What type of access does each employee have? Does the firm use desktop software? Who has access to that software? Who owns that software or is the listed owner? Is that software being backed up? These are serious questions that need to be answered to properly respond if there is data loss, or staff who leave the firm or are fired. Every smart law firm should institute a preparatory list and keep it updated and fluid.

Another process to consider is ensuring the staff at the law firm are using complex passwords as a company policy. It's imperative to protect all data using strong passwords. If the law firm uses a password management system, like Dashlane, who is the administrator? Again, this should be a firm owner. There should be someone at the law firm who manages and reviews the passwords that are selected for the law firm. Passwords should never be password123 or anything that's very simplistic.

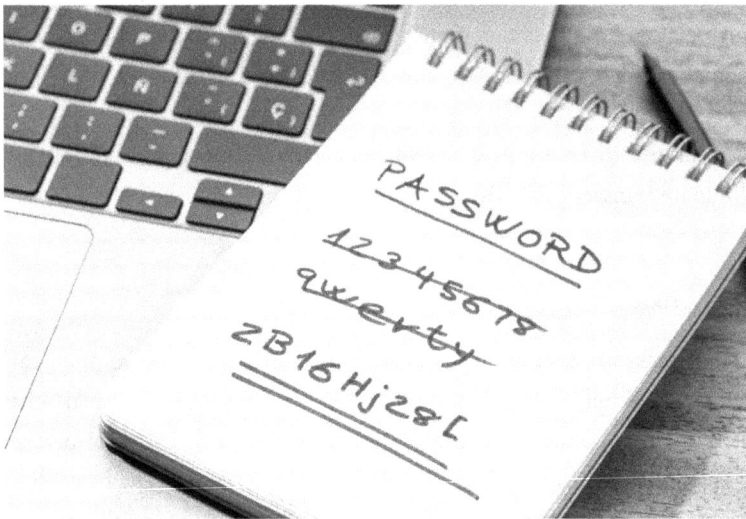

Always select to add multifactor authentication; it should always be added to the login for any program if it is offered in your software of choice.

A firewall is an essential part of any network security system. It prevents unauthorized access to your network by blocking incoming connections. You should also make sure that your router has a firewall enabled.

All computers at work should have antivirus software installed in them. An antivirus program will protect against viruses and other malicious programs that can cause damage to your computer. Malware-bytes is a favorite at our firm because our company uses Mac computers. Norton Antivirus is another good software for PCs.

If you use desktop software in your computer, you need to update it regularly. Updating software regularly will ensure that you have the program's latest version and that it works properly. If you are using Chrome as your browser, you may have to login or relogin if you see that it says "paused." Chrome is constantly updating for the best security, and it's best to ensure you're logged in properly.

Educate employees about security issues. E-mail is typically the number one place that the cyber threat begins. A good first line of defense against cyberattacks is educating employees about security issues. Educating them about potential dangers will make them more likely to report suspicious activities to you. This education includes teaching your staff how to open e-mails and not click on things that seem suspicious. I have seen e-mails that look exactly like they came from Intuit/QuickBooks that are false and most likely sent by unscrupulous people.

The best way to avoid this drama is if they have software for client communication in document exchange. We use Liscio at our firm and are very happy with the platform.

It is imperative for every law firm to have some protocol in place. Let's not forget about the critcal topic of cyber insurance. It's a must in the array of insurance a business should have. Having a plan and a list of who uses what software and what level of access they have is key to a successful law firm being well protected. Let's face it, no one wants to be hacked or have a ransomware attack. Being ready for any situation is paramount.

Focus on Improved Practice Efficiency

There are moments when technology seems to be a time-consuming obstacle to efficiency. But those moments can usually be explained by our human limitations in understanding and using them. When they perform as intended, technological tools will always add to our workplace efficiencies. Every law firm will be competing with another firm—and if that competitor is better versed in the use of the latest technology, it will be an uphill battle.

More Price Competition

Has your firm ever been "squeezed" by either a potential or an existing client? Have you been asked to meet a competitor's pricing? If you haven't yet, you will. The open market is full of firms willing to undercut you for the business. And your customers are savvy. If you aren't taking advantage of efficiencies offered by technology, you may be unable to respond to price pressures in a positive fashion. Manual processing leads to inevitable human error and costly mistakes. You cannot afford to waste manpower and other resources and remain price competitive.

Competition From Non Traditional Service Providers

Legal work provided by non attorney? Yes, this exists already. Look to the state of Arizona where they passed legislation that some legal work can be performed by paralegals and legal assistants. And we've all heard the boast that "I can find a template online and I'll be fine." Not even close to suitable but, to the nonattorney eye, it might work. You might need to be ready to prove that your technology is superior to generic technology.

More Non Hourly Billing

I never thought I would see the day that accountants would be trail blazers in moving toward the nontraditional methods of billing. But we have been! Attorneys are starting to adapt as well. The tradition here can be tricky, and it is important to recognize that shifting from hourly billing will open so many possibilities to the firm. No longer will you be boxed in by eight-hour days times five days per week. And let's face it, no one is capable of billing out that many hours in a work week. In fact, per the Clio Blog named Lawyer Statistics for Success 2022, the lawyers don't collect on 12 percent of the hours they bill to clients—12. The average lawyer billed just two-and-a-half hours (31 percent) of an eight-hour day.

Transition to nonhourly billing is a challenge to more than your systems and processes. There must be solid explanations and answers available to clients and potential clients. They need to know that your value to them goes beyond the hours in a work week. They need to see that your state-of-the-art systems are a competitive advantage not only to the firm but to the client as well.

Corporate Clients Doing More Work In-House

As your clients grow their businesses, they may begin to wonder whether they should hire their own legal counsel and perform certain tasks in-house. It might seem reasonable to think that, if you are outsourcing that much work, it might be preferable to hire and control your own employees to do it. But, if your legal firm has the latest tools and technologies to offer, you can change the game. No longer is it a question of being cost efficient in hiring their own legal staff—your clients can't afford to provide all your tools in a cost-effective manner.

CHAPTER 2

Understanding the Automation Process

Key Questions Before You Begin

Automation can be a fabulous thing. And it's easy to get amped up and excited about the thought of not having to manually key in many transactions. You want to ask yourself several key questions when deciding what would be the best software for you—it won't be the same for every firm.

Accounting Software

Let's start with the base, the accounting software. Accounting software is an essential tool for managing your business' financial data. It can help with basic tasks like invoicing and billing, as well as more complex ones like revenue calculations and project management. It can also be useful for managing clients, reconciling bank accounts, and generating insightful financial reports that can help your business grow.

When choosing your platform, remember it's expensive to move and change products. Finding software that will grow with your firm as your firm adds more attorneys or staff means you need to select software that can measure the metrics. You will need to grow into the software instead of out of the software. When looking at different accounting platforms, look at the bells and whistles. Some may seem unnecessary as you start, but you will be glad you chose software to grow with very quickly. Look at the cost per month or user and determine if paying a little bit now has value so that you do not have to make a major move sooner than planned in the future.

Legal Tech

Using legal technology is a key component of being an effective lawyer. If a lawyer found out that an important case file was missing after arriving at the courthouse, without being able to store and access documents, they would have to return to the office and double-check the file. Having access to the data in the palm of your hand or at your fingertips is critical. The consequences of such a scenario could be devastating.

If you run a smaller law firm but know that in the future, you're going to add staff attorneys, do you want software that will track originating and responsible attorneys? Do you want to track staff production? You may want to track revenue by the practice area. Consider future metrics you may want to track as your firm grows. Write down your list of must-haves and work backward from there. It might also help to have an "in a perfect world" list—including features that may not be necessary today but would be wonderful to have. You might be surprised at the availability of some of them when you are making major changes, anyway.

Are you looking for a program with all the working pieces like document storage, e-mail, and full practice management? Or are you looking for billing software and plan to have the other parts like practice management in a separate platform?

What Efficiencies Are You Trying to Gain?

Efficiency saves time and improves accuracy. There's nothing better than a platform that allows you to work with your billing and track the ready-to-bill expenses waiting to be billed and then can preview a draft or prebill and then approve it so that your legal assistant or bookkeeper can process the billing and push all that data into the accounting platform, Quick-Books. This process can be done manually with many steps or an improved workflow, like the ones in LeanLaw or Clio. No more printing prebills.

Reference: www.clio.com/blog/lawyer-statistics/.

Then, there are efficiencies while getting paid for the legal work. When looking at the ability of a client to pay the law firm with a link by credit card, you will get paid 39 percent faster according to the Clio Trends Report (www.clio.com/resources/legal-trends/). Additionally, there are time savings gained when using the legal software in not having to enter the client's name in multiple places. Did you know that 81 percent of law firm clients prefer to have a payment plan available? Or that 40 percent of legal clients would not hire a law firm that doesn't accept credit card payments?

Again, referencing the Clio Trends Report, firms using multiple technologies collected 40 percent more revenue per lawyer. I don't know how that could not be another incentive to modernize your firm and better use technology in your law practice.

But who oversees defining the process? Is it the partners, the admin, the paralegal, or a combination of these? The answer depends on who is performing the work.

Who Will Define the Process?

This is an age-old question. Who defines the process, and who is responsible for the work? While it's always good to have input from the staff, it's also a good suggestion to inquire from other attorneys about the best process and what they're using in their successful firms. Most people are willing to share the good and the bad stories about selecting the right software. Of course, you can always seek a professional legal accountant or bookkeeper knowledgeable on the topic.

Who Will Build the Solution?

Once you've done the research, now it's time to build a solution. Going from point A to point B or from desktop to cloud-based is quite a leap. Find the right people who know the software. Don't rely only on the developers or sales staff of the software. Make sure you seek out users of the software for the best results. Always test the software in a sandbox environment.

My favorite line is that there's no perfect software. There will be some inefficiencies or areas that are lacking for your firm. There may be a workaround, but you need to know the shortfalls.

What Technology Meets Your Ambitions?

To repeat our earlier question, will your technology fit your firm today and into the future? It all comes down to this one thought. What is your ambition? What are your needs today compared to your needs in the immediate future and maybe five years down the road?

I have always considered technology as a living, breathing, fast-moving thing. Is the software that you're thinking about using ever evolving? Or is it stagnant? Look at what they have on their roadmap. I love good software that provides me access to the roadmap, and it also engages with its users to share their feedback. One of the things I really like about one of my favorite legal technologies, LeanLaw, is that they seek out software users. Not only do they want to hear the attorney's opinion but they also want to hear the opinion of the accounting professionals who live in the software daily.

Six Steps to Efficient Litigation Workflow

Reference: https://pro.bloomberglaw.com/brief/6-ways-tech-aids-litigation-workflows/.

Understand your client: Knowing your clients is critical to a successful workflow. You need to know how to communicate with them. How do you exchange documents with them? How do you request documents from them? Those are the questions you need to answer before you can really find an appropriate workflow, for example, if your firm is a litigation firm.

Evaluate the litigation issues: Ultimately, when you review what's being done in your law firm, you need to review how it's being processed. Where are the areas that can be automated? The attorney will need to draft a complaint. Can you implement software to drive deadlines and dates to keep the entire firm on point with the case or matter?

Attorney/timekeeper productivity: For the firm owner or partner, tracking attorneys and timekeeper productivity is important. Having the right software in place is one of the easiest ways to determine who completes the work efficiently, who does not, and who needs help, and who can offer help to someone else. It's essential data to know to properly run an efficient and profitable law firm.

Investigate the judge's case history with legal tech: Knowing the judge and the judge's history with similar matters will help you analyze how you will present in front of the judge. There are plenty of software out there that will help you investigate the matter and the judge.

Conduct legal research: I'm sure every attorney knows you can conduct legal research online. The most popular resource is Westlaw, which is the go-to place for attorneys to research case matters and legal precedents. Even the most seasoned attorney understands that it's imperative to have solid research skills to formulate that winning argument. Of course, you can still research any argument or matter, or case using Google, the world's number one search engine. Many attorneys start there and continue to a product like Westlaw, the legal library, and any other secondary legal research sources.

Draft the response: There are many resources for finding technology to draft a response. Litera or Lawyaw has great technology to help lawyers prepare drafts electronically. This will help you speed up the process compared to using a product like Microsoft Word. But every journey is different, and it's really what works for the firm and for the individual. Of course, some of the legal software with practice management inside has the drafting capability built in.

Remain aware of risks: The main risk is that you are using antiquated caselaw or irrelevant case law as the basis of your arguments. Look for the red flags in some of the products to see when something is outdated. If you see a red flag, it's probably not a precedent you want to state in your document or in your oral argument.

Automating Law Firm Workflow

Following is an example of my accounting software workflow for law firms.

THE PROPER TRUST LLC

Presented by Artesani Accounting & Mintage Labs, LLC

Dext

Clio
LeanLaw

QuickBooks
Online Advanced

collbox

Relay

liveflow

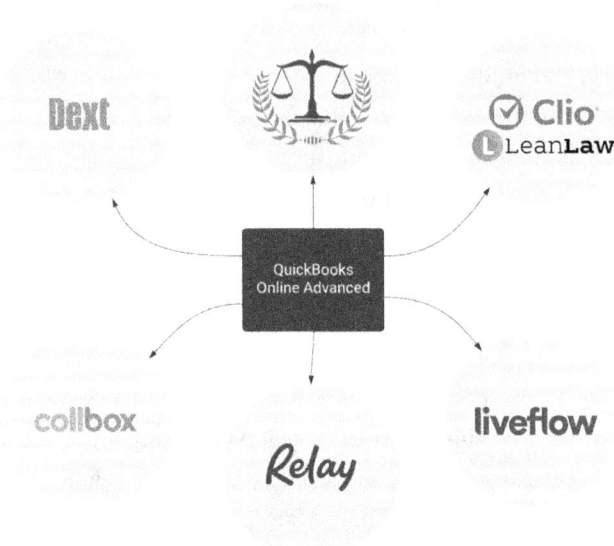

Legal tech automation workflow

Source: Diagram by Lynda Artesani.

Basic Principles

The basic principle of automating the law firm workflow is ensuring all the pieces work seamlessly together. When you start to layer the software, you want to make sure there's no redundancy, and you want to ensure that everything works seamlessly. Additionally, I caution against going overboard and purchasing rarely used software. New software can be a fantastic addition to a law firm, but it can also get addictive when you start to see what's out there. We affectionately call this "shiny object" syndrome.

Process and Resource Optimization

I've seen attorneys change software multiple times, every single year. Remember, no software is perfect. Some things will be lacking in one software that will be better in another. That's why it's imperative to do the research and take the time to figure out what would work best for your firm in your practice area. The advice of a legal accounting professional could be invaluable in helping avoid costly software mistakes.

As an example, perhaps you want to increase traffic to your website. But first, you need to measure the number of visitors to your site and analyze how they got there.

Some useful tools to measure your metrics and results include Google Analytics, which helps you see how many people visited, viewed, and exited pages on your website. It can also track downloads, how long visitors stayed on your website, and other website engagement metrics. Social media channels have their own reporting systems to measure engagement, though you can use social media management systems to consolidate those stats into a single source. You can also use CRMs to gain insight into your marketing efforts. If you don't have a CRM in place and your law practice management software does not provide this sort of reporting, HubSpot or Salesforce are low-cost options that provide basic reporting and valuable metrics.

Automating Lawyers' Document Requests

Software is available to perform many of the functions around document management. Documents can be routed through virtual desks of anyone whose approval is necessary to move forward, missing no steps, efficiently and swiftly. Time stamps and date requirements are handled automatically. Any required follow-up is flagged and appropriately requested. All documents are organized and available as soon as they are finalized. And no one needs to handle a single piece of paper.

Vendor Management

Vendor management is a great place to fully automate your practice. A law firm can devote a lot of time to determining how to track their advanced client and overhead costs. Accounts payable is where Dext can be your new best friend. Dext is a software application that allows you to electronically capture and store receipts, invoices, and other supporting documents that ensure you keep accurate and secure financial records—without the hassle of manual entry. Not only will it help you automate your "money out" but you can also create an e-mail address to have all your bills dropped into the platform. Clogging up your inbox with e-mail bills from vendors can be a thing of the past. And you can preselect the accounts to which they'll be directed.

For instance, let's say you get your monthly phone bill. When the bill is automatically sent to Dext via the special Dext e-mail, it gets pushed into QuickBooks and precoded to phone or utilities. If you have set it up to be paid automatically, it will push in as an expense. If you pay the bill over time, it will appear as a bill to be paid later. No human hands must be involved in the entire transaction. The extra bonus is that the image of the bill is attached to the transaction for easy access and a paperless workflow.

Spend Analysis and Cost Reduction

Any good analysis of where and how the firm spends its money will yield opportunities for cost reduction. But how do you get a meaningful analysis? Automation tools will help you here, as well.

Sometimes you require specialized reporting due to the compensation needs of the law firm. This is where LiveFlow www.liveflow.io/ can help. You can manipulate your data and connect it to QuickBooks, creating some impressive reports and dashboards. Tracking key performance indicators and creating "report cards" for attorney time and profitability provides invaluable information.

Let's talk about realization rates. In simple terms, this is actual hours invoiced divided by total number of hours worked. This is the working realization rate. You can also track the collected realization rate using paid invoices. Your integrated software cannot do this automatically, but LiveFlow can and can also suggest areas of possible cost savings.

Realization rates can be improved by staying on top of recording billable hours. By the end of a busy day, work performed may be forgotten, losing billables.

Clio and LeanLaw are great tools in legal tech that ensure that time is tracked efficiently and online. Both also provide templates to standardize billing language throughout your practice. Creating clear, concise verbiage is a win for the firm. When a customer understands a well-drafted invoice—with as much itemization as possible—they are less likely to complain or seek a reduction.

CHAPTER 3

Why Outdated Software Is Hurting Your Firm

In my business, I run into attorneys who dislike change. They use the same antiquated software year after year and may grumble a bit when they must pay some good money to replace an old server—to the tune of $15K to $20K. Perhaps, they "saw the light" when we could not be in our offices due to the pandemic and discovered how difficult it was to log into that server. Maybe, the old-fashioned firms had to pay unexpected expenditures to an IT person to set this up so workers could access the drive and the desktop software.

While the desktop software may still work, it tends to be inefficient. I have seen firms use billing software like TimeSlips and keep the program as a silo, not integrated with the accounting software. I've seen accountants and bookkeepers then use QuickBooks Online and bank feeds to book the income via the bank feed in a cash basis type of bookkeeping. This method is wonky. It leads to erroneous entries and is not the correct way to validate the data. Most desktop legal tech do not have complete accounting, and the ones that do have it is a minimal viable product (MVP). They have basic reporting where attorneys will miss out on the best financial reports to run their law practices.

When we moved a client off PCLaw, the administrator, Mary, was not 100 percent sold on QuickBooks and LeanLaw. She had the process of PCLaw locked in. We had to convince her that not only was the program crashing, causing Mary to consistently restart her computer multiple times in the day, but also that the workflow processes required much more effort and time.

The Experiment

We had Mary record a retainer for a new client in PCLaw to prove our point. This process required her to set up the client and matter and enter the retainer as a deposit. We counted 11 clicks to complete the entire transaction. Next, we had her do it in the new workflow of QBO and LeanLaw. Three clicks were all that was required with LeanLaw. It was then that she had her lightbulb moment and realized that if she had to do this multiple times per day, there would be significant time savings for the firm. Once she mastered the new software, she was well on her way to efficiently using her time and gained more time in her day to do other tasks.

Remember, desktop software can be pricey. Support programs that go along with the product can be an additional fee. Add to that the server, IT person, and increased chances for a data breach with this type of workflow, and it is easy to see why you would switch to the cloud. Your data is safer than in a vulnerable desktop setup, accessible to all on multiple devices. Don't let old clunky software slow your firm down.

Do You Know Your Installation Date?

The "Your software may be out of date" pop-up is a browser notification that alerts you that your software is outdated, and you need to download an updater. However, if you download the supposed "updater," this installer will install various potentially unwanted programs and adware programs on your computer. So, if you see any browser pop-ups promoting a software updater, it is best to close the window and not install the offered program.

To find the installation date of programs on a PC:

- Search for "control panel" in the Taskbar search box and click on the respective result to open the Control Panel.
- Click on the Programs and Features option.
- If it is not visible, set the View as large icons. Once in the Programs and Features panel, locate the app and check the Installed-On column.

This column will show you when the app was installed on your computer.

To find the installation date of programs on a Mac:

- Click on the Apple logo at the top left corner of your screen.
- While holding down on the "Option" key on your keyboard, select "About This Mac." This will change to "System Information."
- In the System Information window, scroll down the list on the left pane and select "Installations" under the Software section.
- This will show you a complete list of all software currently installed on your Mac.

Risks of Outdated Software

Crashing computers was a daily occurrence, sometimes numerous times per day. As mentioned before in my story about Mary and her PCLaw software, the firm initially contacted us because they were experiencing a crashing problem. The staff had to stop when the program froze and restart the system. When they reached out to the folks at PCLaw, they told Mary that the firm needed to upgrade the program and pay an additional $15K to have the software support plan.

They used an outdated version of PCLaw for years and were in the 2014 version. There was a significant price increase to get them to the current version.

Think about it. Would you use an eight-track tape or a Walkman in your life today? Why would you use antiquated software for your business needs?

Decreased productivity and lost time: Another reason you want to move to a more modern workflow is that with the older desktop software, there is a decrease in productivity. If your office staff is experiencing slow load times and unresponsive programs are a regular occurrence for the firm, it may be time to change.

Your software and programs may be outdated, causing your productivity to suffer. The time you spend waiting for things to load can add up, and it's probably more than you think. If you have hundreds of files all over your computer with clear organization, it is easier to find the exact files you need. With proper search and organization tools, your staff will gain valuable time that they could spend working on other priorities.

Metrics: One of the main disadvantages of using old technology is that it severely limits your business's flexibility, including data analysis and communication. The new software will allow your business to stay on track with analytics, giving you a better understanding of employee and company performance. Additionally, old and new technologies often need to work better together, so forget about mobile capabilities. Seriously, who doesn't look things up on their mobile devices today? It is the computer in the palm of your hand.

Vulnerability: Legacy systems can pose a severe security risk for companies if they're not kept up-to-date. Most companies try to mitigate this problem by regularly releasing security updates for at-risk software. However, once a system is no longer supported, it won't be able to receive these patches and updates. Using a system that is not supported can lead to disaster recovery and backup solutions issues as they become outdated and difficult to manage. When your data security is at risk due to failing equipment and systems, it's time to refresh your technology.

Tech's Fast Pace: Short Software Life Cycle Depends on Updates/Upgrades

I don't have to look further than my new Tesla to see where technological changes have benefited us. The car is jam-packed with tech that might scare some away. Some features were still relatively new when I wrote this book. You can look at the distance this car can go on one charge. That distance is in the 350-mile range. The battery is where they have made some incredible improvements. My first Tesla was ruined in Hurricane Ian when the flood waters rose to over three feet in my garage. Any chance of salvaging the vehicle was instantly wiped away by her condition. The seats were back, and the windows were open. That is a safety feature if the car is ever submerged.

The self-driving is a bit tricky and still in beta. But it is cool to try it out. The car can drive itself quite successfully. But you have to be fully in control of the vehicle. I expect this technology to improve over the next few years.

Similarly, the same goes for office technology. Do you still have a fax machine in your office? I am guessing not. Today, there is a world of electronic signatures and pdfs. Everything is instant. Just think of all the processes you may have done manually in a word document; today, many of these tasks are automated.

Does the change seem fast? I think so. Just look at some stats from Media Peanut:

- **Computer chip cost**: A chip with 2,000 transistors cost $1,000 back in 1970. Today, the same chip costs $0.02 to manufacture.
- **Number of Internet users**: There are 4.88 billion as of the fourth quarter of 2021. The rate of Internet adoption expects to exceed 61 percent in 2022.
- **More data than ever before**: About 89.7 percent of big data has been generated within the last two years.
- **How fast is AI growing**: By 2025, data center spending on AI processors will grow by over four times. The Global AI market is forecasted to hit $89.8 billion.

- **Cloud solutions increase**: About 69.2 percent of spending for tech is forecasted to be spent on cloud solutions.
- **Smartphone usage**: Millennials unlock their smartphones 71 times per day, while Generation Z unlocks their phone an average of 82 (MediaPeanut 2021 survey).

With cloud-based software, you are always in the best version. But when using desktop software, you are at the mercy of the software update. I have worked with clients afraid to do the update because they didn't "want to mess things up," so they kept ignoring the constant warning that the software update needed to be performed. These updates are put out for a reason. There can be minor changes, vulnerabilities, or holes in the software that need to be plugged to protect your data. The changes and updates are fluid.

Outdated Software Can't Integrate With New Applications or Run Smoothly on New Devices

LeanLaw is the most streamlined and efficient legal software that only integrates with QuickBooks Online. I would be rich if I had a dollar every time a potential client asked me why LeanLaw doesn't integrate with Quick-Books Desktop. I must explain that LeanLaw works with QuickBooks Online only. LeanLaw is heavily invested in being the best legal technology, which aligns differently from QuickBooks Desktop. Intuit, the maker of QuickBooks, is heavily devoted. Look at the innovation in QuickBooks Online, the Advanced version, and see where they are working to improve the program. Each year, more and more changes make our job easier.

Additionally, each year, more legal technology hits the market. There are thousands of applications out there. Most law firms are looking for technology that they can access from the palm of their hand with their mobile device.

No Patches Are Available If Vulnerabilities Are Found

Software vulnerabilities are one of the most common ways ransomware is delivered. Unpatched software not only makes it easier for malware to get in but also makes it more likely. In some cases, when software needs to be updated correctly or patched, attackers can access networks without having to harvest credentials. Once in the system, they begin attacking essential programs and viewing or exfiltrating sensitive data. Additionally, many types of ransomware have evolved to forms that are difficult to detect, therefore extending their dwell time for maximum destruction.

Easy Prey for Advanced Cyberattacks Using New Technology

Cyberattacks are made using a type of malicious software by cybercriminals. These sophisticated cyber groups consider creating these viruses and malware as a business to prey on unsuspecting individuals or companies. They spend days or months watching and studying their victims. They do their reconnaissance. They do their research right down to knowing your details from looking at you on Facebook. Remember, these crimes are lucrative.

There are red flags. These criminals try to create a sense of urgency. The most popular way they infect your computer and system is through e-mails or text messages. Take your time to verify and make a phone call to ensure that it is accurate. Look at the "from" on the e-mail. Look for bad grammar or typos in the e-mail. If your Spidey senses are tingling, you should investigate it or click on the e-mail before you go further. Do your due diligence, even if it means a delay in responding to a suspicious e-mail. It's easier to explain a late response than mop up after a cyberattack.

Ransomware

If a computer or network has been infected with ransomware, it blocks access to the system or encrypts its data. Cybercriminals demand ransom money from their victims in exchange for releasing the data. After an infection, victims of malware attacks have three options: pay the ransom, try to remove the malware, or restart the device.

Paying the ransom is not recommended as it only encourages cybercriminals and does not guarantee that your data will be released. Removing

the malware yourself is also not recommended, as it can be challenging to do and you may damage your system further.

There are so many different types of malware and ransomware. Some will lock you right out of your computer, and some will lock you out and threaten not to release your data if you don't pay a ransom via bitcoin. It can be truly devastating to your firm.

We have encountered a few firms that have been "held hostage" by cyberattacks. The firms scramble to keep working, and the client data, especially personal data, is of the utmost priority to keep safe. Downtime from a cyberattack can be a tough pill to swallow, and a process is imperative if your data is compromised.

Here are a few great resources for reporting breaches and keeping on top of known vulnerabilities:

Ic3.gov

This site is the federal bureau of investigation's (FBI) Internet Crime Complaint Center and an incredible resource for staying on top of the reported cybercrimes. They provide up-to-date consumer alerts and industry reports. Being aware is the key to stopping these issues from affecting your firm.

Stopransomware.gov

Of course, protecting your law firm and instituting best practices before a technology breach is the most important. Also, a government site, this one will provide you with a place to report ransomware attacks and be informed of any known vulnerabilities.

Outdated Software Lacks Ransomware Protection

Outdated software can cause many headaches for users. It can't run smoothly on new devices, and it can't integrate with new applications. Outdated software can be a big problem, especially if you rely on that software for your work and sensitive client matters.

There are also security risks to consider when using outdated software. If vulnerabilities are found, there are no patches to fix them. Obsolete software makes the software a much easier target for cyberattacks. These attacks can come from malicious humans or simply from the increased chance of system failure.

Outdated software is not equipped to handle modern-day cyber-attacks, putting any data you use, store, or have access to at risk. Your systems will be more vulnerable to ransomware attacks, malware, and data breaches without updated software that can protect your information.

The many devices connected to your law firm network could contain viruses leading to major business disruption.

Too many devices and not knowing what each user can access is a recipe for disaster. You can do a few things to help prevent insider threats and utilize some best practices:

- During regular security training sessions, teach your employees about the dangers of unintentional and intentional insider threats.
- Set up contractors and other freelancers with temporary accounts that expire on specific dates (e.g., when their contract ends).

- Install employee monitoring software to help reduce the risk of data breaches and intellectual property theft. This software can help identify careless, disgruntled, or malicious insiders.

Outdated Mobile Devices Using Your Network Can Contaminate It With New High-Tech Viruses/Ransomware

The use of mobile devices in the workplace is commonplace. Organizations are increasingly finding it challenging to keep up with the demand while ensuring that their security systems are up to date. With how often cyber criminals exploit outdated systems to carry out large-scale attacks, it's not hard to see how using ancient mobile devices could pose the next significant cyber threat for companies. Criminals have already developed malware that takes advantage of these weak areas of older mobile devices.

FEMA: Four Out of Ten Companies That Suffer Data Loss End Up Closing

There is a fantastic resource with case studies and tips on ensuring that you and your business are prepared for the "what ifs" if you lose data due to natural disasters. FEMA has an excellent document to review; you can access the pdf here (www.fema.gov/sites/default/files/documents/fema_fema-331-protecting-business-operations.pdf). As someone who has lived through a significant hurricane in Southwest Florida, I can tell you firsthand that having your workflow in the cloud can save your company. We had a major flood in my home and office. We had to move to another location. Because my workflow is cloud-based, I took my laptop and did not skip a beat with my clients and business.

Size of Threat Substantial: According to Avast, 55 Percent of the World's Software Packages Are Out of Date

To conclude, this is a serious topic that every business owner should address and prepare for. According to research by security company Avast, around 55 percent of software installed on PCs across the globe is in the form of an older version of the application. That number is rising. That means there are a lot of vulnerable computers out there, and they are easy prey for cybercriminals.

Outdated Software Horror Stories

Do you remember Windows XP? When Windows XP was first released in 2001, it was a popular operating system. However, Microsoft stopped providing security updates for the software in 2014, which made it vulnerable to cyberattacks from malware and ransomware. For example, the WannaCry ransomware attack in 2017 used a Windows XP vulnerability to spread quickly across computer networks, causing damage to businesses and organizations worldwide.

Vulnerability to Hackers/Fraud Increasing

Did you know that 95 percent of all cybercrimes are due to human error? Yes, that's a real statistic.

We worked with a law firm that actually had Desktop QuickBooks and was recently hacked and paid ransomware to get their data back. The criminals locked it. What was astonishing to me is that the client didn't seem phased by this. It was almost like an "oh well" moment. In fact, there was some pushback about using our program Liscio to communicate. Yes, we invest in a product to keep data exchange between our firm and the law firm safe; Liscio keeps the data secure.

Eventually, the client adapted to our system. How many other firms experienced similar issues?

Since the pandemic, there has been a *300 percent* increase in cyber-crime. This is likely a reflection of the increased remote work.

According to the blog Teknologiz, the average ransomware attack costs a firm $223,000, with an average of 19 days offline where the firm is unable to work or function. And as if these statistics aren't scary enough, 94 percent of all malware attacks are started in your e-mail inbox. You click on an unsuspecting link and you're done.

Some of the bigger cyberattacks are as follows:

Yahoo had the biggest one with 3 billion users affected. The criminals got your password, your birthdate, and a lot of other data that you don't want to share. You may have been using that on other sites, which is the hope by the cyber criminals.

Uber is another; 157 million profiles of drivers and passengers were stolen in that attack.

Here are a few of the major famous ones regarding law firms being hijacked by cyber criminals:

Resource: https://arcticwolf.com/resources/blog/top-legal-industry-cyber-attacks/.

Grubman Shire Meiselas & Sacks

In May 2020, Grubman Shire Meiselas & Sacks, which offers legal services to the entertainment and media industries, acknowledged having experienced a ransomware attack. The hackers leaked information involving Lady Gaga, who is a client of the law firm. They also threatened to release information involving other celebrities.

The attackers asked for a ransom payment of $42 million to prevent the release of the documents to the public. The perpetrators originally asked for $21 million, then doubled their payment demand.

News outlets are reporting that the criminals behind the attack received $3,65,000 from the firm. They threatened to release additional data, which includes information about celebrities, if they didn't receive payment.

Oleras

In 2016, a cybercriminal using the alias Oleras allegedly targeted 50 law firms to steal confidential information to facilitate insider trading. The hacker attempted to hire accomplices via the criminal underground to help breach the law firms' defenses and then use keywords to search for pending deals.

To entice others to join, Oleras advertised a plan that detailed the names, e-mail addresses, and social media accounts of the law firm employees to be targeted.

One of the phishing e-mails associated with the scheme appeared to originate from a business journal asking to run a profile of the recipient about their work in mergers and acquisitions.

Cyberattack type: Phishing
Location: The United States
Cost: Undisclosed

Once made aware of the threat, the FBI initiated an investigation and issued an industry alert. To date, none of the law firms targeted by Oleras have disclosed a breach in their firm's defenses.

And this last one just made my heart sink. This is one that happened to me recently when a law firm just e-mailed me their W-2s that were processed by a prior bookkeeping firm:

Jenner & Block and Proskauer Rose

Jenner & Block admitted that in response to a request that appeared legit-imate, the firm had "mistakenly transmitted" employee W-2 forms to "an unauthorized recipient" in 2017. The phishing scheme resulted in the inadvertent sharing of personal information of 859 individuals, including their Social Security numbers and salaries.

Proskauer Rose experienced a similar attack, involving what appeared to be a routine request from a senior executive within the firm. In this case, the firm lost control of more than 1,500 W-2s.

Cyberattack type: Phishing
Location: New York
Cost: Undisclosed
People affected: 2,359

E-mailing sensitive data was the main reason why we, as a firm, did not want to have e-mail communication with our clients. We just deal with too much sensitive data. Liscio was the answer and still is today for us to communicate securely.

Examples of New Threats Related To AI And Blockchain

As AI has automated more and more decision-making processes in different industries, it becomes more vulnerable to exploitation. Adversarial attacks are one example of how AI can be tricked—for instance, by changing an input image like a stop sign into a speed limit sign. Another example is deep fakes, which are fake videos that look and sound like the real thing. Deepfakes are fake videos or images that are created using AI algorithms. They can be used to spread disinformation or to impersonate individuals in order to commit fraud.

Cyberterrorism Against Law Firms

The year 2016 was the year of the Panama Papers leak. Hackers breached the computer network of a Panamanian law firm, Mossack Fonseca, and gained access to over 11 million documents. These documents revealed the firm's involvement in offshore tax havens and money laundering schemes.

But it is not just the legal industry, the medical field has also been breached:

Ransomware attacks have been a growing problem in recent years, as they exploit vulnerabilities in outdated software to encrypt and hold patient data for ransom. In 2017, the British National Health Service

(NHS) was targeted in such an attack, which caused the cancellation of more than 19,000 appointments and operations.

And in 2019, the American Medical Collection Agency (AMCA) suffered a data breach that compromised the personal and financial information of millions of patients from various medical firms that used its services for billing and collection.

And not to be forgotten, accounting firms have been attacked.

Accounting firms are often targeted by cyberattacks due to the confidential client information they keep on hand. In 2017, Deloitte was targeted in such an attack, which exposed e-mails and intellectual property. The hackers gained access to the company's e-mail system through a single administrator account that was not protected by two-factor authentication.

In 2021, Wolters Kluwer experienced a ransomware attack, which disrupted their cloud-based tax and accounting software. This caused many accounting firms to be unable to access critical client information.

Lack of Continuing Vendor Support

In highly competitive tech, companies go out of business frequently or are bought out, with new management.

There are a couple of things you should consider when determining whether or not to keep using an app that is no longer supported by the vendor. One is the presence of security vulnerabilities. If the app presents too much of a risk, it may be time to discontinue use and find another solution. Another thing to think about is what alternatives are available. If there are other apps that can do what you need without the same security risks, it may be worth switching to one of them.

If the app is essential to your business or personal needs and you can't rely on it anymore, you may need to find an alternative solution. You can research and compare alternative apps that offer similar features and functionality to the original app and choose the one that best fits your needs.

Make sure to back up your data before making any changes. You can export it to a different format, like a spreadsheet or database, and store it safely.

If you're thinking about buying an app, it's important to do your research first. Find out if the current owner plans to continue supporting the app or not. You can check the developer's website or social media pages for updates, or contact them directly to ask about their plans for the app.

User Interface Complicated, Time-Consuming

If you find new software but the user interface is too complicated, there are several actions you can take, as follows:

- Spend some time exploring the software and familiarizing yourself with its features and functionality. This can help you get a better understanding of how the software works and how it can be useful for you.
- Look for tutorials or training materials. Many software companies provide tutorials or training materials to help users learn how to use their software. You can check the software's website or user manual for tutorials or training materials, or search online for video tutorials or guides.

If you're struggling to use the software or find the user interface confusing, reach out to the software vendor's customer support team. They can help you troubleshoot any issues and offer guidance on using the software more effectively.

Some software programs let you customize the user interface to make it more user-friendly. You can check the software's settings or options menu to see if it offers any customization options, such as changing the color scheme or rearranging the layout.

CHAPTER 4

Data Security

Key Data Security Principles

When it comes to data security principles, it boils down to this:

- Technology: Keep your programs up to date.
- Access: Limit user access to only the areas that they need to be accessing.
- Authentication: Two factors, if available.
- Documentation: Know what users are using and what software is used at the firm. Document this and implement an action plan if things go wrong or someone leaves the firm; plan if there's a breach.
- Confidentiality: This is critical for compliance.
- Education: Educate your staff on suspicious e-mails and protocol.

Basic Precautions

Great Backup Procedures

Whether you are using desktop or cloud software, a good backup should be in place. For desktop software, storage of the data should be in a secure place and not on the same computer housing the data. For cloud-based systems, most have a way to dump data into a comma separated values (CSV) file. Additionally, programs like QuickBooks Online Advanced have their own secure data backup system. It's included in the pricing.

Backing up the data should be part of the workflow process and not done randomly. Regular backups are key. If you ever have to redo data due to a loss, you are learning this lesson the hard way.

Use Good Anti-malware and Antivirus Software

Antivirus software is created to protect against malware and viruses that could potentially damage or infect a computer. It's important to have this type of software installed on your computer as it's one of the most critical investments in a household or business. If your antivirus software is unable to remove malware, a standalone malware remover will be able to do so.

It's important to run an antivirus scan on your computer regularly to help protect it from malware and other threats. However, it's also important to use a malware remover to eliminate any malware that might already be on your system. Using both an antivirus program and a malware remover will give you the best possible protection against all types of threats.

Antivirus Software or Malware Remover—The Key Difference

Antivirus software is a crucial tool for preventing the download of virus-laden files onto your computer. It also works to prevent the activation of viruses, should they somehow be downloaded onto your computer. By keeping these files from being downloaded in the first place, you can avoid any potential problems.

If you download a file that is flagged by antivirus software as malware, the software will prevent any damage to your system. However, the infected file still needs to be contained and deleted.

How to Choose Anti-malware, Antivirus Software

Not all antivirus software is created equal, so many factors must be considered.

There's nothing worse than trying to browse the web only to have your computer slow down because your antivirus software is taking its time to scan everything.

Choosing the right antivirus software is essential to protect your information from cybersecurity threats. However, with so many options on the market, it can be difficult to know where to start.

When choosing antivirus software, the best place to start is by looking at the protections it offers. Antivirus software should protect you not only against viruses but also against other threats as well. At a minimum, your antivirus software should protect you against common dangers to your privacy and safety.

There are many types of cyber threats you may come up against, such as:

- **Malware**: Unwanted software programs that can infect your devices and either disrupt their use or collect data from you. This category of threat commonly includes viruses, spyware, adware, and ransomware.
- **Scams**: Deceptive schemes that trick you into revealing sensitive information or allowing malicious access to your device. These typically come in the form of e-mails, websites, text messages, bad apps, and online messages. Some common scams to watch out for include spam, phishing, and pharming.

Your antivirus software should protect against the most common types of malwares and prevent them from infecting your devices. Make sure you have real-time prevention that will stop threats before they can do any damage. And if your computer does get infected, you'll want rapid removal of the malware to get your system back up and running as quickly as possible.

Make sure your antivirus program offers both proactive protection and rapid infection removal to keep your devices safe from all types of threats.

Threat prevention features in your software should include the following:

- **File scanning**: This will scan new files for any dangers before you open them. It compares the file against the antivirus' full database of known risks to decide if it is safe.
- **Complete system scans**: These will review every corner of your device for any compromised data. This can help you be sure that nothing is lurking around undetected.
- **Web browsing protection**: This filters URL links and web pages to judge their safety history and level of potential risk. Internet security is pivotal to your digital protection.

Threat removal should be included in all antivirus systems. Just be sure that it quarantines potentially malicious files to allow you to review them.

When browsing, be sure you're choosing a true "antivirus" that offers prevention and removal. Other products like those dubbed "anti-malware" may only offer removal without preventative features.

Discussion of Some Good Anti-malware/Antivirus Software Products

You can't go wrong with some of the known companies, like Kaspersky, Norton, and McAfee, to name a few, that work well with Windows products. They've been around for years and are good solutions for software that will help you keep your data safe.

Additionally, if you're using a Mac, the software is different. You must keep your Mac up to date when you see that little red number on the gear in your settings. I like to update my Mac in the evening, as some of these updates take time.

Some users of Mac computers think they don't need to worry about antivirus, but that's not the case. All the abovementioned companies provide software protection for a Mac. There's also a Mac keeper, which is a software I use. It does the same scanning of your files as if you were on a PC. It will just keep a healthy running computer.

The Importance of Updating

As mentioned before, you must keep your operating system secure. When you see that notification, it's easy to click ignore because you know it's going to take some time to do it. Most computers have a way that you can schedule it for the evening. Set your system up to automatically notify you of any updates. These updates are generally installed because of a threat to the system. There may be a weakness or a vulnerability that is being discovered and protected.

Security Measures

Two-Factor Authentication

I know, I know, two-factor authentication is a pain. It's that extra step that can be annoying and time-consuming. But it's an extra step or layer that protects you from cybercriminals. Some two-factor authentication is a text sent to your phone to verify that you are who you are. Some require an authenticator with a set of rolling numbers that you must save on your phone and just enter. I like this one because it does protect you from the problem of being cyberattacked.

Encryption

Encryption is a technique used to protect data or communication from unauthorized access. When data is encrypted, it is converted into a code that cannot be read by anyone who does not have the key to decrypt it. The process of encryption and decryption is known as cryptography. In computing, unencrypted data is also known as plaintext, and encrypted data is called ciphertext.

Examples: Encryption is a process of transforming readable data into an unreadable format. This is done using a mathematical algorithm and a key. The purpose of encryption is to protect information from being accessed by unauthorized individuals. The data can be stored on computer systems and transmitted via computer networks. It is often used for private messaging and financial transactions where security is paramount. People use encryption to increase the security of their communications. Additionally, encryption can be used to verify the authenticity of the sender and receiver of messages, as well as to ensure that messages have not been tampered with during transit.

Other Security Measures

Something you may not have considered at your firm is the security of the employees. Workplace safety and violence prevention should be central to any law practice management system. All law office employees should be trained to recognize and manage threatening, potentially dangerous individuals. Client-facing staff like your receptionists or legal professionals need tools to protect themselves and prevent early-stage situations from escalating into major, dangerous events.

Protecting Your Staff

It is essential for receptionists to have a clear view of the entrance into the office, particularly doors, elevators, and all traffic areas, so that there are not many opportunities for people to sneak in or hide. Make sure that the front desk is designed to provide a barrier between receptionists and clients but still allow easy exit. Delineate clearly what clients are permitted to do in the lobby and front desk area, so that they understand where they are allowed to go.

Make sure that any office objects that are potential weapons are removed from the front desk and should be stored in drawers or cabinets; staplers, scissors, letter openers should all be kept out of sight of the public. Computer screens and family photographs should also be kept out of sight.

Train Staff

All attorneys and staff members handling clients should be trained in how to deal with angry or hostile behavior. This includes learning de-escalation techniques, how to redirect negative behavior, how to set boundaries, and being aware of assault risks. There are many free online resources and security consultants who can provide this training. Continuous practice will help employees to hone these skills.

Article to credit: www.attorneyjournals.com/10-safety-tips-for-law-firms-attorneys-and-legal-professionals.

Passwords

Password Managers (Software)

Password Protect: This is our firm's secure software that protects our client's passwords as well as our firm's passwords. Practice Protect was built for accountants but could be used for law firms as well. This is pricey software that is not easy to implement but is highly secure.

1Password: With 1Password, your data is safe and encrypted. Not only is the password encrypted but also your browser history and your sensitive information like your name and address.

Dashlane: This software has a business enterprise offering that is easy to use. The user interface is intuitive, and your employees can easily set this software up for their computers and phones. It is proactive and will alert your staff to any breach where the user should change the passwords. This can be done simply in Dashlane.

Browser password managers: This would be your Google password manager, which works on Chrome or Safari's password manager and auto saves passwords on your Mac computer. These are typically turned on by default when you log into your Google account or when you set up your Mac. To access the list, you have multiple layers of security to reach to see the saved passwords.

You may be wondering why I did not mention the popular Last Pass software. There was a major breach of this software back in December 2022. You can read more about this breach here: https://blog.lastpass .com/2022/12/notice-of-recent-security-incident/. I used this software and abandoned it due to the severity of the breach. Most users not only saved their passwords in this software but there was an option to also save credit card details. The program was easily shared, which made it a great tool for firms to share a login that was cloaked from the person it was shared with; however, the breach was significant. The notification from Last Pass was slow to the users and left many of us exposed.

Password Security Tips

One of my favorite security recommendations is to make sure your passwords are complex. Use a service that will create them. You could use a phrase as well. Try not to reuse the same password. There are companies that will help you generate them. It's free unless you want it on multiple devices, which I highly recommend. But there are many password-generating companies and services out there. And even some for children. You probably never thought about your kids, but they may have their software on your computer, and they need to have secure passwords. It is called Dino pass.

Data Security Audit

Key Elements

Ideally, audits should be performed, minimally, annually but more likely quarterly or semi-annually. The partners in the firm should get together and, with the help of an assistant, map out a few key items.

Depending on your goals, you may want help creating automated workflows that audit, flag, or share data in standardized formats. Depending on your specific needs, data quality, data management, or data integration software could be an ideal solution for your business. A few items to consider:

- How is the data being stored?
- How is the data being maintained?
- What software are you using to communicate with clients?
- Is the data secure while exchanging documents?

Schedule/Timing

The word audit tends to scare everybody. Nobody wants to go through a tedious audit as they are time-consuming. But want to or not, they are important to do. It's better to be safe than sorry, as the old adage goes.

There should be an annual audit done by the firm's partners with the help of a reliable employee or an outside auditor.

When Is It Best to Use an Outside Consulting Auditor?

Data audits can help your business by investigating and resolving big issues—such as security and customer data accuracy—thereby reaping benefits and avoiding future problems.

Data security is of utmost importance for businesses of all sizes—recent high-profile breaches affecting companies, organizations, and even cities are a testament to this. Furthermore, legal compliance has become a major consideration in the wake of regulations such as the California Consumer Privacy Act (CCPA) and the European Union's General Data Protection Regulation (GDPR). Lastly, data storage is another significant area of concern for businesses of all types.

Data is increasingly driving business decisions, so it's essential that teams have full faith in their data. An audit improves not just the accuracy of your data, but also could uncover silos, access issues, or areas where more collecting would be beneficial.

How to Choose an Outside Data Security Auditor/Consultant

Cyber security consultants play an important role in today's business world. They help companies protect their data by looking at all levels of their computer systems and how they interact. In order to be effective, cyber security consultants must have a deep understanding of computer systems and how they work.

It's always great to get a referral to find a good data auditor. That might not be an easy thing to do, but if you ask your colleagues, especially the larger firms, they may be able to refer someone to you.

You can always turn to the website G2 (www.g2.com) for software reviews as well as finding a cyber consultant. This website is my go-to for tech searches. Take the time to look at the ratings and read the reviews. Finding the right firm is critical for the health of your firm, and finding a good cyber consultant will keep your company safe.

After evaluating a consultant's reviews on G2, check out the software by doing a Google search and read the reviews for more opinions to assist you in finding a good one.

Law Firm Special Considerations

ABA 2024 Legal Technology Survey Report: Depending on the year you are reading this book, you will want to follow this annual report as it will provide you some trends on security and what other attorneys are doing. According to the 2022 Legal Tech Report survey, 75 percent of all respondents reported having some type of technology training available at their firm. Technology training increased along with firm size with 32 percent of solos having training available at their firm, followed by 64 percent for firms of 2 to 9 attorneys, 79 percent for firms of 10 to 49 attorneys, 93 percent for firms of 50 to 99 attorneys and 100 percent for firms of over 100 attorneys.

Data security staff training/maintenance: I'm glad the ABA chooses to include this topic in their report, especially as it pertains to budgeting for staff training. Training time is a crucial part of any business, and though it can be costly, the investment is always worth it in the end.

Phishing is a big problem when it comes to data breaches. According to the 2021 Verizon Data Breach Investigation Report, it was present in 36 percent of cases. But phishing isn't just a problem for businesses—over 90 percent of cyberattacks begin with a phishing e-mail aimed at individuals. And the problem is that most people can't even recognize a phishing e-mail when they see one.

Client confidentiality: A key rule that lawyers must follow is that they cannot share information about their client's case without the client's permission. This rule helps to ensure that clients can trust their lawyer to maintain confidentiality. The importance of cyber security training and insurance for law firms cannot be overstated. Client confidentiality is of utmost importance, and this training should be set on fixed dates on the law firm's staff's calendar.

Fiduciary duty: Law firms are often targeted by hackers because they store valuable and sensitive information. They may also have access to trust accounts that contain their clients' money, making them susceptible to theft or ransom. To protect themselves, law firms should take steps to secure their networks and data.

While resolutions are important, firms also understand that it is their ethical and professional duty to protect their clients' data. If a breach occurs, firms should report it as soon as possible to the relevant bodies. The ABA's Rule 1.6: Confidentiality of Information requires lawyers to make reasonable efforts to prevent the inadvertent or unauthorized disclosure of client information.

Requirements from new data governance laws: There are data privacy laws in place in virtually every country regulating how information is collected, how data subjects are informed and what control they have over their information once it is transferred. Failure to follow these laws can lead to hefty fines, lawsuits, and even bans on a site's use in certain jurisdictions. Legislators have proposed many laws governing data privacy in the United States, but none have been successful. The American Data Privacy Protection Act (ADPPA) is the furthest along of any predecessor, but it still has a long way to go. At this point, it's unclear whether the act will overcome the challenges it faces or succumb to them.

Contributing article: www.osano.com/articles/data-privacy-laws.

CHAPTER 5

The Virtual Firm

Virtual Lawyer Trend

A virtual lawyer, is it possible to be one? Just work from home and not have to work at a law firm's office or go to court? For some types of law practices, this has become a serious trend. Copyright or patent law firms can certainly be an example of that. A client can reach out and ask for help on their patent, and the research and all the work behind this type of law can be practiced from home.

The Virtual Law Firm Trend

If you just think back to a few years ago, most law firms were of the brick-and-mortar type. The clients would call the receptionist and then drop in for a visit in person to discuss their case.

The pandemic certainly did a lot to shift the movement toward the virtual law firm. For an industry that was set in its "paper-centric" ways, the pandemic did a lot to push it forward. Many attorneys we worked with did not even know how to use Zoom to meet with clients. Once Zoom court was a thing, it became an easy shift to having meetings with clients virtually. One benefit of this is that we can record the meetings.

It is truly learning the new software and embracing it. Once attorneys realize that there is a better way, why not? There are incredible time savings to this method. No travel, no waiting rooms. More billable hours! Of course, the way we do business shifts and changes—for the better. The virtual world includes virtual meetings and virtual documents. Most of the documents are stored in the cloud for easy retrieval by all parties. This shift is a win not only for the lawyers but also for their clients.

ABA: *Virtual Is the New Law Firm Realty*

While it may seem like a new concept, the ABA contends that virtual law firms have existed for 20 years or more. The fact that the public is unaware of this, may be evidence that it works well. Large, successful virtual firms have everything to offer that a brick-and-mortar operation has, except the physical office and its upkeep and expense. If you research law firms online, you might be surprised that it's difficult to tell the difference between virtual and traditional firms. Like many other industries, practicing law is moving seamlessly into this space as potential clients become increasingly comfortable with it, especially younger ones.

How to Start a Virtual Law Firm

Starting a virtual firm is like starting a regular firm. You must create a name, order the FEIN number and licenses, get your bank accounts in order, and market your new firm. You should order software like Quick-Books Online or Xero. Meet with an accounting professional to get you set up and started.

Establish yourself and tell the world! Most attorneys we have as clients are starting out this way. They may leave a large firm and have an agreement with their existing firm to take some clients to their new firms to get started. I can honestly tell you that these lawyers were so happy to get started this way on their own. They never look back in that rear-view window and think, "what if?" They just go for it! And they are very happy and successful soon after their leap of faith.

What Does a Virtual Law Firm Look Like?

We worked with a client who had created a superior virtual firm model. The office space owned by this large firm was small and shared among its 40+ attorneys. This full-service law practice handles all types of law.

Although there were four main equity partners, the rest of the attorneys were the non equity type. These attorneys figured out a plan to compensate the rainmakers and service all types of clients. Even though the individual attorneys worked from home, they could pay their share to rent the main office space. Expenses were allocated too.

They mirrored a large Manhattan law firm if you landed on their website. They dazzle you with the services they provide and the wide array of types of practice areas. The best part of the scenario is that these attorneys figured out how to make this practice work. If another attorney was needed for their expertise, that was easily handled within the virtual walls of the firm.

It goes without saying that a premier technology app stack is what keeps this firm working cohesively. These attorneys do not have the water cooler discussions but can do a quick Zoom meeting to collaborate on a case.

Challenges of Running a Virtual Law Firm

Ethical questions: There are ethical challenges for both employer and employee in a virtual workplace. Both need to be certain to ensure confidentiality for clients, for example. In a traditional workplace, someone in the firm knows who is using company space and resources. But is the virtual employee sharing a desk and computer with a spouse or child? How secure is the firm's—and the client's—data? Is there a plan in place to guarantee that all firm information is captured, stored, and maintained appropriately?

Productivity: Employers not used to virtual work environments may be concerned about their remote employees' productivity. Early in the pandemic, employers without remote operation experience were justifiably concerned about worker productivity. Few of us—employers or employees—knew how that would work. We didn't know the tools and systems available to assist us. We didn't know what was expected. We didn't know how to do it. But, as in many things, we got better at it as time went on. We found that Zoom meetings might even be less stressful than in-person. We learned how to manage time and work uninterrupted when we needed to do so. We learned that we liked the time and financial savings involved in giving up the commute. Some workers have concluded that they feel they are more productive—at least in the short term—when allowed to complete projects remotely. But monitoring remote productivity is not without its challenges. Some employees are more affected by the loneliness accompanying it than others, impacting productivity negatively. Over time, employers must find ways to stay connected to staff and encourage a team attitude that can evolve in shared space but not in individual remote workplaces.

Wellness: Working from home has unique benefits and challenges, and your employees may still need some time to adjust. Early in the pandemic, many of us talked about having extra time because of the foregone commute—and we planned to use it for exercise. And some of us did that—while others ate more, gained weight, and felt worse for it. Remote employees must be encouraged to take appropriate breaks and care for themselves. The worker taking a Zoom meeting while sitting in bed may not be a poster child for wellness!

Fraud: One thing that caught me off-guard after the pandemic was the fraud among some of the law firm office staff. When they were told to come back to the office, I was surprised to see how many people resisted. I later found out that some of them had been working for multiple companies at the same time and couldn't keep up the act when they had to be in the office. Ethically, this could not be maintained and with talking to the law firm partners, most suspected this was happening as the return of work product dropped significantly when the suspected staff members worked from home.

Confidentiality: The most important step in ensuring confidentiality is to institute a companywide policy on document security. Training of staff to be careful where they log in is also important. Make sure they do not use public Wi-Fi when doing their work on the road.

Practical Challenges

Most of the challenges surrounding a virtual firm are the ones we see from not having that human contact. Nothing beats a room full of lawyers at a conference table collaborating and strategizing the tactics of a case.

Another important consideration is that you need a staff adept in using the software required to run a virtual firm.

Tools Required

You need great software to accomplish a completely virtual firm. A few required suggestions:

1. Clio: Fantastic practice management software.
2. LeanLaw: One of the BEST legal billing software with tons of reporting and metric tracking.
3. MyCase/Cosmolex: All-in-one software for accounting and practice management.
4. Zoom for meetings.
5. Zoom phones.
6. Office 365 or Google Suite for collaborating.
7. Docket wise.
8. Practice-specific tools.
9. Litera.

The ABA also provides an updated book you can purchase with a list of attorney tools for working from home: www.americanbar.org/products/inv/book/424883450/.

CHAPTER 6

Identify Your Tech Stack

How to Inventory and Evaluate
Your Existing Technology

I recommend conducting an inventory of your app purchases and recurring subscriptions at least once a year. It's easy to get caught up in paying for monthly subscriptions for apps we think we need, but sometimes these apps can fall short of our expectations. Or, we may already have stopped using them but continue to pay for them. When looking at your expenses, it's essential to have a category for software so you can more easily identify which items are recurring. If you don't have this category already, I recommend adding it and then going through all your vendor transactions to find the recurring items. Some may be inexpensive, but even an app at $9.97 per month can add to an unnecessary expense.

Inventory worksheet: I created a software inventory worksheet so that you can keep track of software for your law firm and evaluate any new technology. Here is a link (https://bit.ly/software-analysis) to the google sheet.

Annual Inventory Worksheet for Software

Software Name	Description of Purpose	Used for Procedure	Authorized Users	Cost of Software	Similar Product	New Software Pricing

Source: Photo of an inventory worksheet created by the author, Lynda Artesani.

Evaluation worksheet: I recommend doing a simple survey from the users of the software on your team to see if your staff is finding the software useful or beneficial. Survey Monkey has a simple template you can use to aggregate this information and do a complete evaluation of the software currently in use. You can access this template here (www.surveymonkey.com/templates/software-evaluation-survey-template/).

Reviews of Top Legal Workflow Software

LeanLaw: I recommend LeanLaw to any mid-market firm looking for outstanding legal billing software as their cloud solution. It is considered a Premier app with Intuit QuickBooks for a reason. It has a seamless connection to the accounting platform.

The software is not only affordable but also comes with a lot of features that can really help automate your law firm's processes around billing, and more importantly, with that size firm, you get fantastic reporting. Even if you're a small firm with only a few attorneys, I believe this software would benefit you because it can help simplify your workflow. As accountants, we love the two-way sync as it really automates tracking your client expenses, so none are missed.

Practice Panther: This cloud software is pretty, but that is all I can say about it regarding trust tracking. The reconciliation process is very weak and easily broken. If you use a credit card to pay for client expenses, there is no way to track that in Practice Panther.

Lawcus: This software is abundant in features for the attorney and the bookkeeper. I had a meeting with the owner of Lawcus, who showed me a demo of the product. He's excited about creating a fantastic program that is relatively inexpensive compared to the others on the market. It has a cool dashboard and uses Google and Google forms for intake forms. It's rather like a combination of LeanLaw and Clio. It has integrations with Google and Microsoft 365.

Cosmolex: This is an all-in-one cloud solution and is one of the few cloud-based systems the court uses when there is a trust infraction. Why? Because the platform is extremely rigid. If you must make a change to a transaction, you have to undo your bank reconciliation all the way back to the changed transaction. In other words, it is not as forgiving. Another thing to note is that it could be more intuitive and may require you to use the help to search for solutions. On a positive note, it has a good three-way bank reconciliation and pretty good reporting.

Clio: Clio is a wonderful well-established software for a solo law firm because of its strong integration capabilities. It can seem pricey, but it has everything you need in one space and that must be factored into the cost of the software. You get more. The Dashboard is beautiful, and the timeline is very helpful for accountants. This is the granddaddy of all legal software, and it really shows when you look at all the features. We recommend it for small firms. The only downside is that the reports could be better, but they are working on improving them.

We've been collaborating with Clio to enhance the system's reporting tools. They just released a beta of the three-way reconciliation, and we're excited to see how this new feature can streamline the process for users. This feature is still a work-in-process. While Clio does offer reporting capabilities, they often come at an additional cost—something from an outside firm. I think it should be included in the base program especially given how integral getting accurate reports are to law firms.

There are a few things to keep in mind when using Clio software, one of which is reconciliations. It's important to reconcile monthly. Another thing to remember is that if an attorney makes even a minor change to an invoice, it will create a separate transaction for a transaction that's already inside QuickBooks. This is because Clio has a one-way synchronization with QuickBooks. Despite these few items, we highly recommend this program—there is no perfect software, and Clio is an excellent choice and our preferred software.

Adding Clio Grow to your law firm's software suite is a great way to track your leads from beginning to end. This software includes a great metric tracking system to help you identify any weak points in your work-flow and comes with intake forms to automate the entire process.

MyCase: MyCase is unique because it offers two different types of software. There's the QuickBooks integration add-on software that's been around for a while, and then there's the new all-in-one program. The all-in-one program has a lot of financial backing, so it's something to consider when choosing software for your firm. However, because it's new, there are a few things that could be improved regarding accounting features.

The design of the new platform MyCase is like QuickBooks. You don't need QuickBooks for the all-in-one product. The company is investing a lot to make improvements and wants accountants' input on making this a stronger accounting platform. Attorneys who used the older MyCase program, a billing platform integrated with QuickBooks, preferred it because they felt it did a better job handling communication, time tracking, documentation, timelines, and other client information.

Evaluating Legal Workflow Software

Advantages: Evaluating your legal workflow software or process is important and should be done at least once a year. Workflows and software change rapidly, so it's good to take the time to see if any automation can be done to update your process. Outdated methods can hinder productivity, so ensure you use the best and most current workflow possible.

Disadvantages: For every positive, there is a negative—and the same goes for change. I often see attorneys who are quick to change their software every year but need to realize how costly and time-consuming this can be, not to mention disruptive to the office's workflow.

As a rule of thumb, people don't like change, so attorneys must resist the temptation of every new, shiny object that comes their way. Rather, they should take the time to evaluate the cost of the new software and its implementation and migration before making any decisions.

Other Considerations

Fit for Company Culture?

The age of your team is something you should take into consideration when thinking about what type of software to implement within your company. As we get older, change can be difficult and disruptive to our workflow—so it's important to choose software that will cause the least amount of anxiety and disruption for your staff. A peaceful transition is the key to success here.

Staff Training Issues

Staff training is an important topic that often gets overlooked. Training new staff or retraining existing staff can take a lot of time and effort, but it's important to do it right first.

When we do a data migration for a client, we usually take a phased approach so that everyone knows what's happening and their part in the process. We also don't just abandon the law firm staff once the project is complete—we stay on to help troubleshoot and answer any questions that come up. We stay on a minimum of one month during the crossover month, and most of the time, we stay on through two billing cycles.

It's important to remember that anybody can be easily trained. And since everybody learns differently, it's important to provide different options for training material like written instructions and videos. Also, successful training usually happens when it's delivered in small, bite-size chunks so that people can retain the information more easily. Remember that when you're attending training, you're still expected to do your work—you can only dedicate some of your time to learning the new program.

Ease of Use

Most cloud-based software is user-friendly these days, but just in case, it's always good to know where things are located within the software. For example, all transactions and processes in QuickBooks are located under the + sign. You'll see the same in Lean Law. Any one-time transactions or settings are located under the gear icon. If you select software that's been around for a while and isn't as user-friendly, you might find that it will slow down the training process.

One of the suggestions for doing training on any new software is to get software called LucidChart. LucidChart helps map out how the new software works, and even if a team member only does one segment of the work, it's always good for them to see the entire workflow in one place— visually. This allows for better communication and collaboration among team members so that everyone is on the same page, working toward the same goal.

Reliability

Reliability is important to consider when choosing software for your business. You can use a program like Downtime Detector to see how often a particular piece of software is down and check its uptime percentage. For example, if QuickBooks goes down, you can see which parts of the country are affected and how long the software has been offline.

Error Recovery

When it comes to error recovery, it's important to have a backup system in place. Just because your data is stored online doesn't mean that it will always be available to you, and you should have an emergency plan in place in case of outages or other unforeseen events. QuickBooks Online Advanced includes a built-in backup system for the monthly subscription cost, but not all software programs include this feature. If your software doesn't have a backup system, you should consider paying extra for a reliable backup service, especially if your accounting data is critical to your business operations. I like the product Rewind (https://rewind.com) for backing up your accounting software.

How Frequent Are Updates?

Another key factor to consider when choosing software for your business is how often the company updates its program. In today's world, it's essential for companies to keep their programs updated to avoid any potential cybercrimes. All software should be updated for new features. When speaking with a salesperson from a software company, be sure to ask this question so you can gauge how well they keep up with industry standards.

Evaluating Vendor Support

When evaluating vendor support, it's important to consider whether you'll have access to a live person if you need help. A chatbot that simply sends you to a help page is obviously not a great solution when you need help. When comparing software, look to see the support hours, if it has a chatbot or a text platform that includes a live support person.

Customer support options vary depending on the vendor. Some common options include e-mail, phone, or chat support. Some software vendors only offer support through tickets. Additionally, support can be either freely available or paid. Asking a vendor if the support has a price tag is an important consideration. PCLaw, for example, has a hefty price tag for support and is not inclusive when purchasing the software.

You also want to avoid contacting your legal billing software company for accounting support—that's not their job. Even if you use QuickBooks Online, support can help you with questions on implementing the software but not with accounting questions.

Look at the hours their support is available. Some have business hours, and some companies are open seven days per week. If a tiered system is in place, how long do you have to wait to hear from a live person?

Monitoring Software Performance/Upgrades/Maintenance

I typically go to the website Down Detector to research the reliability of the software. This is for the big players only, like Intuit/QuickBooks.

Costs to avoid: There are three main types of costs associated with implementing a new project management tool.

- **Initiation costs**: These include retiring the existing system or keeping it operational during transition.
- **Setup costs**: These fees cover hardware and software acquisition and implementation.
- **Ongoing costs**: These costs are incurred yearly and include items such as server maintenance, annual upgrades, technical support, and administrative training.

Best Software for Small Law Firms

The Clio Manage and Clio Grow software packages are excellent choices for practice management software for your law firm. I highly recommend them for the smaller one- to two-person law firm. In addition to its features that aim to increase efficiency, productivity, and profitability for law firms, Clio is a leading provider of cloud-based software solutions tailored specifically for law firms.

In addition to time tracking, billing and invoicing, client management, document management, and task management, Clio Manage is a comprehensive practice management system. Their software has the advantage of being easy to use, customizable, and able to integrate smoothly with many other software applications, including Microsoft Office, Google Drive, and Dropbox.

Clio Grow, which is a separate additional software that you can purchase as a package for your law firm, is an extremely powerful CRM tool that allows law firms to handle their client intake process, track leads, and automate the marketing process. To gain insight into the effectiveness of their marketing efforts, law firms can streamline their intake process with Clio Grow, capture leads from their website, and track their marketing performance.

Best Software for Medium to Large Law Firms

Having used LeanLaw for a number of years, I can strongly recommend this piece of legal software as one of the best options for attorneys needing billing software. As a leading provider of legal software, LeanLaw offers a comprehensive solution for managing billing, invoicing, time tracking, trust accounting, and other functions essential to law firms.

The user-friendly interface of LeanLaw is one of the key advantages; it makes tracking time and creating accurate invoices very easy for attorneys and their staff. Designed specifically to meet the needs of legal professionals, this software integrates the best with QuickBooks Online Advanced, which gives you the robust accounting system every larger firm needs.

There are a variety of advanced features in LeanLaw, including the ability to track expenses, create custom invoices, and run financial performance reports. It also helps attorneys to stay on top of their finances and make informed decisions by providing real-time insights into billable hours, expenses, and outstanding invoices.

In addition to providing outstanding customer service, LeanLaw also boasts a team of knowledgeable, responsive, and helpful representatives who can answer any questions you may have or assist you in any way you need.

One item that is a small drawback is if you are going to create a three-way reconciliation in LeanLaw at the end of the month. It is recommended that you download that excel spreadsheet from the Trust Report housed inside LeanLaw on the very last day of the month. We have this as a regular task on the last day in order to preserve that detail. There is no way to print a report for trust on an "as of" date as the data comes from QuickBooks itself.

I highly recommend LeanLaw to any law firm or legal service provider looking for an efficient and effective attorney billing software.

CHAPTER 7

Adjustments to Make in a Post-COVID World

Office Versus Remote

Law firm leaders see that their workforces are becoming hybrid or split, with some workers coming to the office, some working remotely exclusively, and the majority doing a combination of the two. Managing such a diverse or split workforce has its challenges. The challenges come in the form of data security, firm culture, attorney advancement, client confidentiality, client service/responsiveness, technology, logistics, and fair compensation.

As someone who has worked with their fair share of law firms, I often come across an owner who demands that the entire staff return to in-office work full time. When Covid hit, it was a massive wake-up call to the legal industry to stop being so antiquated in their software selections. One only must look to social media and Elon Musk's Twitter or Tesla to see that he requires the staff to return to the office or get a new job (https://fortune.com/2022/11/10/musk-orders-all-twitter-staff-back-office-first-company-wide-email-exceptions-need-personal-approval/).

Upgrading and enhancing one's workflow can be beneficial for many reasons, as the experience of law firms still using what they have used for many years shows. As the Clio legal trends report from 2022 points out:

Before 2020, the median number of days that lawyers spent in the office was about 14 days per month, which fell to just eight days at the start of the pandemic. The rest of 2020 saw lawyers spend far fewer days in the office, and 2021 saw only slightly more office use. In 2022, lawyers still spend fewer days in an office overall—about 13 per month—compared to 2019. In comparison, nonlawyers (e.g., paralegals and administrative staff) spend more days in the office, but we still see declines in the relative number of days spent in an office.

How office use has changed among four groups of law firms

Average % of firm staff working exclusively from an office

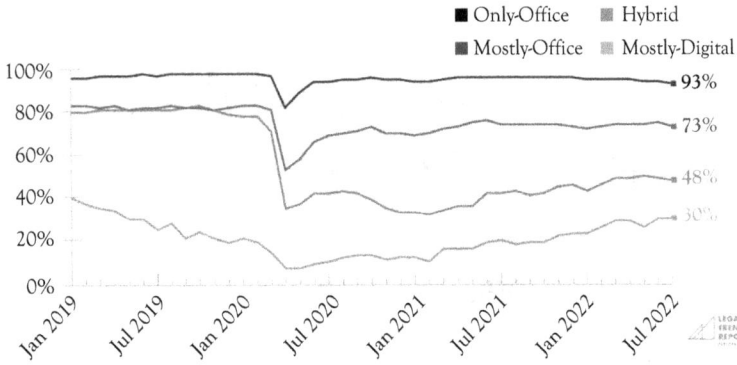

Source: Office use graphic: Image credit: www.clio.com/resources/legal-trends/2022-report/read-online/.

> *The most dramatic shift in office use appears in the Hybrid group, which comprises 10 percent of all firms. Before 2020, more than 80 percent of all firm members in this group worked exclusively from the office. By April 2020, this number dropped to just 35 percent. Not only did this group see the most significant drop in office use during the pandemic but it also saw fewer firm members return to office in the months and years that followed. By mid-2022, fewer than 50 percent of firm members were working from an office.*

What Can Be Done Remotely

There's a growing trend of virtual paralegals and legal assistants. For the latter, it really depends on the person running the firm. Someone with a mindset of being completely virtual can adapt to having a legal assistant work virtually. They can hold Zoom meetings to work effectively, like working late in an office. Obviously, secretarial work can also be done remotely. There are plenty of resources out there for less expensive remote staff, where they're outsourced and are contracted workers.

What Cannot Be Done Well Remotely

Obviously, all court sessions were remote during the pandemic, but many of them have returned to in-person. I remember speaking to a death-row defendant attorney during the pandemic and about how difficult it was for her to convey her case via remote and put up a strong defense. She felt she lost the ability to connect with people and convey the emotional side of her case. Any attorney who must be in court can only really do this remotely if the courts dictate that. A lot of that went away after the pandemic.

Receptionists are the first people that clients see when they come into an office, so they must be able to communicate well and provide assistance as needed. This is especially true for immigration firms, where clients may not speak the same language as the receptionist. Receptionists, therefore, need to be able to speak the client's language to provide quality customer service.

How to Manage Remote Office Staff/Attorney

The biggest concern for attorneys and anybody who runs a remote business is whether their employees will clock in and work when they're supposed to. The temptation when they're working from home is to suspect that employees can claim that they're working even when they're not. That's the part that terrifies business owners.

The best way to manage this work is to have a system in place. Whether you work remotely with them or not, you must have expectations around the work produced, and a time frame is imperative. Accountability and production of work will be a resource. Also, much of the necessary human interaction is impossible with remote work—you're talking to a computer screen. Setting up a time to not only adjust work but produce a way to provide human interaction can help alleviate some of those challenges.

Every Friday, we set up a time to meet with staff to discuss their families and have general conversations with them. This can be done in a group setting, but it's also important for the business owner to take an interest in an employee or contractor's life from a personal side. It not only allows them to vent any frustrations they might have but also keeps them in the loop of things going on with the company and opens them to new ways of doing things.

It was eye-opening for me when a staff member was out, and no one had the time to cover their position. I had to jump in and help our client, and I quickly realized how out of scope this job was. My staff person was helping the client with things that were not a part of the contract.

Revisiting the workflow is something you need to review with a staff member. Having them write up their job description at least once a year is a good idea, so you know everything they do for your firm. It's critical to have this information.

Client Contact

Pros and Cons of Remote Client Contact

For introverts, communication via computer is much preferable to face-to-face contact. This is because they feel more comfortable in a space where they are not physically meeting the person they are talking to. Although this method has some disadvantages—such as missing out on important cues that can be picked up through body language—there are also many positives, like not having to travel to meet with a client. This can save a lot of time, especially if you work in criminal law. Often, when meeting with a client in person, there is more to the conversation than just work-related topics.

Managing Zoom Client Conferences

We all laughed hysterically when the attorney logged into Zoom and told the judge that he wasn't really a cat. I watched that video so many times when it first came out because it always makes me laugh.

But for Zoom, you want to have a great background and great lighting. The background should be professional, and you should try not to use a virtual background if you can. Obviously, if you're working from your bedroom, you want a tastefully done background. There are plenty of options available online.

If you have the option to go with professional office space, it's usually the best route. At the beginning of the pandemic, when everyone was using Zoom for meetings, it seemed like every attorney I worked with had the same boring bookshelf background.

I had one client who had a great sense of humor about it. He repeatedly heard me complain about the same background that all attorneys use—that standard bookshelf—so he decided to see if I was really paying attention. He set up a stripper pole and had a girl in a bikini dancing behind him during our next meeting. Needless to say, he got my attention! We had a great rapport after that, and although he was only a client for a data migration project, he remains unforgettable.

Maintaining Client Trust

Sense of humor aside, we've all learned that we can't trust everything we see online. Our clients and prospects all know this as well. Humans rely on our instincts about who and what we can trust, and it is very difficult to exercise those instincts virtually. Do you buy clothing online or want to feel the fabric and touch the item first? Once you know and trust a vendor to deliver, you probably wouldn't hesitate to buy from them virtually. But they need to earn your trust by delivering the quality you expect before that happens.

Selling your services is no different. You must prove yourself to be the competent, capable, and trustworthy professional the client expects. Once you've done that, you've earned their trust, and working in a virtual space becomes easier. You still need to deliver on your promises, but that virtual "wall" between you won't be an obstacle.

Should You Increase the Frequency of Client Contact?

In my opinion, we should consider having more client contact because we are working remotely.

It's too easy to put our heads down and work, not communicate with the client, and just keep working. But when you do that, you miss out on a lot of important information. For example, do you know that your client is refinancing their mortgage and will need the data immediately? Do you know what pain points are present in the office itself?

A lot of our financial meetings with our customers are done weekly or monthly, depending on the scope and size of the firm, so it's important to communicate with them so that you can be prepared for anything that comes up.

This is also true for attorney–client relationships. If you read the latest Clio Trends Report, you'll see that the number one complaint from clients is that attorneys don't communicate with them. They feel ignored. Setting up a schedule of regular communication sessions with clients is critical for creating a happy client experience. And remember, a happy client experience equals referrals.

Handling Problem Clients

No one likes dealing with difficult clients, but unfortunately, they are a reality that most of us must face at some point in our careers. If you have a remote client who is giving you grief, it's important to try and handle the situation delicately, as you don't want to drive them away entirely.

First, find out why they are a problem client. Is it because they need to provide you with the necessary documentation? Or is it because they constantly call your office and take up much of your time? Once you pinpoint the root of the problem, you can start working on a solution. Perhaps you can set up some ground rules or limits concerning communication or frequency of contact. The best way to avoid having problem clients in the first place is to meet with them before officially taking them on. This way, you can get an idea of their communication style and whether they will be a good fit for your business.

CHAPTER 8

How to Adapt and Get Your Staff to Accept Technology

Introducing New Technology to Staff

When introducing new technology to your staff, always be delicate and expect some resistance—especially from employees who have been with you for a while. From my experience working with multiple law firms, I've found that the older generation may resist change while the younger folks might be excited about it. Of course, this is just a generalization and doesn't have to be the case every time.

Dos and Don'ts

The best way to approach this would be to consider making this a group effort and decision. Ultimately, the decision lies in the hands of the firm owner, but it's important to involve the staff in determining what will work best with the software implementation. An excited team is more likely to be ready for change.

Create a roadmap and big picture for your team. Offer up a few software options to make the decision collectively.

It's important to explain to your staff why you're changing the software, whether because the legacy system is no longer supported or because you're looking for ways to automate some workflows. With this new technology, some staff members may feel fearful about change, especially if they think their jobs might be threatened by automation. Remind them that if this change means their jobs change, it could give them roles involving something more important to the firm. This should help alleviate any fears or concerns about the change. Employees who feel valued will want to help you make the best use of their skills.

Allocating time in an employee's schedule to learn new software is crucial to success. They must know you think the process is important enough to devote resources—their valuable time—to do it right. It's better to learn the new technology over time and in shorter bursts instead of trying to learn it all at once. This way, employees will better understand new systems and software and be able to use them more effectively.

Don't assume that staff already knows how to use new software or that it is similar enough to what they know that they'll easily transition. Don't get frustrated with them if they struggle.

Changing to Cloud-Based Software

If transitioning your company to cloud-based software, be aware that this change can take time for some team members. Employees may need time to adjust to using the new software as the concept can be dramatically different.

Be patient and have clear expectations for your team. Again, I cannot state this enough, explain the reasons for the change and help employees understand how the new software will benefit the company. Assist those who struggle with using the software and provide resources for learning more about its features and capabilities.

When new software is introduced, it often creates new workflows. Make sure to schedule regular meetings to review progress and give staff a chance to document any hiccups or weaknesses they encounter. This is especially important for new software, as there are bound to be areas that need improvement or updating that you will only be aware of if you give people a chance to voice their concerns.

Don't be too forceful when communicating this to staff—nobody likes to feel like their job is on the line. Instead, try to sound positive and supportive. Let them know that you're committed to making this work and that you value their input.

Having review meetings, a month after implementing changes in your company is always a good idea. This is a time to check in with staff, see how they are doing and if they have any questions or concerns. It's also an opportunity to see if anyone needs more training.

Yes, we have seen cases where people we have trained default to the old software because they're more comfortable with it. This is not ideal because it takes twice as much time to do the work this way. These review meetings are incredibly important to see if the software works as described and if the team is working together fluidly.

Introduce Tech in Steps

When introducing a change, whether big or small, it's always important to take a careful and thoughtful approach. For example, if you're starting from the idea phase, it's crucial that everyone on your team is on the same page and knows exactly what the plan is step-by-step so that the change can be executed smoothly. I've seen training go poorly because staff members were only trained in the segment they would be working in without any prior knowledge of the rest of the project. As a result, they felt lost and confused because they couldn't see how their individual task fit into the larger picture. However, when staff members are given a chance to see the big picture and how their task is just one small part of it, they usually have a moment of realization where everything clicks into place. Not only is this approach more successful but it also feels more meaningful to those who are carrying out the change.

Evaluating Vendor Staff Training Programs

I've seen effective and ineffective training methods while working with various software companies. Liscio, for example, is a secure messaging service and file storage company that did it right when they onboarded my firm. They set up multiple short 15-minute sessions to train us in various aspects of the platform, which was very helpful.

In contrast, I've been in other training sessions that were less effective. The trainers just flew through the material and the steps without taking the time to explain things properly. The new users felt exhausted and confused at the end of the day rather than excited about the new and improved workflow.

As you conduct regular check-ins with your team, take some time to evaluate how the vendor's training is going and if it's a good match for your needs. We recently did a training with a company specializing in contract writing, but the vendor representative who showed up was based in Canada and needed the product to demonstrate that it was U.S.-based. This caused some major problems since we're unfamiliar with the Canadian version of their product.

She corrected herself at the next meeting; it was obvious that she was still a little shaken from our first meeting. That first meeting didn't go well, but she made up for it in the second. But then, when we started using the new software, it went wrong. I know that sometimes people just don't mesh well. This firm assigned a sales onboarding person to our firm, but it was clear that they should have done their homework. He was condescending and provided no value whatsoever. Needless to say, I didn't feel very good about the situation.

I initially wanted to scrap the entire idea of using this software. But we didn't do that, we reached out to the person who recommended the software and they put us in contact with a different onboarding specialist. What could've been a disaster—and a huge waste of everyone's time— turned out very well. But this can even happen to someone who is very well-versed in technology. At our staff meeting, we discussed how that first onboarding session went so poorly and how we could resolve the issue, whether we scrap the software or change to a different onboarding specialist, the latter being what we chose in this situation.

When to Seek Outside Assistance

Taking charge of your situation and being proactive separates a good onboarding experience from a great one. If you're ever feeling unsure or like things could be going better, it never hurts to reach out to someone with more experience for help or guidance. They'll be able to help you assess the situation and figure out what changes, if any, need to be made for the onboarding process to run as smoothly as possible. This is especially important when it comes to new technology because it can be difficult to know what's not working and what is. When you get feedback from those who have gone through the process, you can get some clarity. By debriefing after each session, you can ensure that everyone involved feels comfortable and confident with the new system—which is the key to a successful onboarding!

How to Plan Staff Training

In-Person or Online Videos?

As someone who has experience with both methods, I can say that I believe live training is important as it helps us to gauge where everybody is in terms of learning the new technology. Having videos to refer to will also be beneficial in the long run because it will serve as a valuable resource during the learning process.

There isn't one method that is better than the other, they both have their own benefits. It's important to remember that people have different learning styles and types. Many older folks do well with a book or a PDF guide, while the younger generation loves shorter videos. I think all people do well with live training as long as it's not too long—a two-hour session doesn't help anyone because people lose attention. However, having that live session and opening it up to Q&A is important, so you get that one-on-one training.

Overcoming the Pitfalls of Remote Staff Training

A common issue with remote staff training is low engagement levels. However, there are a few ways to overcome this. One way is to ensure that everyone has their camera on during the training, as this will make it seem like you're all in the same room together and help with engagement. It's also important to encourage interaction by perhaps doing breakout sessions or exercises in small groups so everyone can participate.

Handling Questions and Regular Follow-Ups

One of the best tips I can offer to ensure successful training is to provide your client with a slack channel where they can ask questions on an ongoing basis. We do this often with our training program, and we're successful because it allows someone to get help right away when they get stuck. The interaction on the slack channel is great, as many people can track what's happening in the different areas we're training for. This way, people can get the help they need promptly and effectively.

We have accounts receivable channels, accounts payable channels, trust channels, and channels for any clients needing extra help using the new software. We call it a support channel because we want to ensure our clients are successful in data migration. For some firms, like criminal lawyers or collection agencies, the different scenarios that may pop up are important to successful data migration. You can even include a weekly or monthly check-in meeting to ensure everyone is on track.

Evaluating Training Effectiveness

How often: The frequency of evaluation for training effectiveness depends on the timeline. If training is fast-tracked, then evaluations should be more frequent. If training is introduced in bite-size moments, evaluations can be spread out. We recommend weekly or biweekly evaluations as we go through the training process.

Get feedback from staff: It's important to get staff feedback during training on the new software—this will give you a better idea of how it's being received and what needs to be changed. Sometimes you'll find that people are initially resistant to change, but if you can get to the root of the problem, you may be able to diffuse any negative feelings. For example, if someone says the software is terrible and takes twice as long as the old process, you can ask why and find out that they thought it would be faster. Once you know that, you can provide more training or reassurance.

The next question you'll want to ask is, why do you think the process is slowing you down? If the person answers that they are working slower at figuring out where to go and what to click, you can ask another question to get more information. Why are you slower? Do you need more training? Do you need to review the course material in the onboarding process? By asking why five times, you can get to the root of the problem and see if there's anything that can be done to speed up the process.

When you ask the five "why" questions, you may find that there is a valid reason for the complaint that goes deeper than the software issue. It may be a training issue. Asking the five "why" questions can help you understand where the problem lies so that you can solve it.

Key parameters to measure: As you evaluate training, you'll want to consider how well the staff is progressing and if they're meeting your company's standards. Time and accuracy are important measurements to look at. Additionally, check that all advertised features are being used and that any ecosystem or layers of software are working together smoothly. Security protocols should always be adhered to.

Red flags indicating problems: Any time you're thinking about integrating new software into your business, it's important to look out for red flags that might indicate the software isn't working as it should.

Does the software integrate well with other programs, as it claims? If not, are you finding it difficult to get support from the software development team? The same goes for the onboarding team—are they responsive to your questions and concerns? If you notice any of these red flags, it's important to research them before selecting a new program to avoid any future headaches.

Getting Manager Buy-in and Support

Software changes can be a big undertaking, especially when staff is different from the management team who originally came up with the idea to switch. Maybe a staff member saw an opportunity for efficiency and automation. Regardless of where the idea came from, you'll need to get management on board before anything can happen. This can be difficult because changes usually create some friction and come with expenses— which may only sometimes be budgeted for. A good way to start is by evaluating the potential savings and benefits of making the switch. If it makes sense from a financial standpoint, you can begin to make your case to management about why this would be a good investment for the company.

To get the management team on board with your new software, you'll need to position it as a positive change for the company. Define why the software would benefit the company—does it improve accuracy? Speak to process improvements? Or is the company in need of some modernization? By clearly outlining the benefits of the software, you'll be able to garner excitement and support from your management team.

Evaluating New Product Effectiveness

I include the software report card because it breaks down the specific points you should look for as a positive when evaluating any new programmer platform that you're implementing at your firm. The rating scale for software applications goes from 1 to 5, with 1 being inadequate, 2 being poor, 3 being acceptable, 4 being good, and 5 being excellent. Remember there is no PERFECT software. You must weigh the "must haves" with the software's features and determine what is best for your law firm.

Free app scorecard via google form

Source: App Scorecard, photo of google form made by the author.

Scheduling Regular Evaluations

Evaluating the purpose and use of your software is just as important as evaluating its costs. Sometimes software can just end up lagging and needing to be updated. To avoid this, it's important to ensure that your software is always developing and keeping up with recent technological innovations. Technology changes incredibly quickly, so you should evaluate your software at least once every year to ensure that everything is working together smoothly and that your ecosystem is modern and up to date.

Key Questions to Ask

There are some general questions to ask when evaluating your software and systems. Do you remember what problems you hoped to solve when you implemented it—and does it do what you'd hoped it would? Are there unexpected barriers to effective and efficient use? Have your needs grown and changed, and has the software kept pace? How well does it integrate with other software and systems in use? What is its cost in terms of time spent troubleshooting, working around, retraining, and maintaining? Is there some capability missing, something you thought it would do but cannot or does not do?

Market Survey: Is Better Software Now Available?

Many attorneys need to catch up when it comes to this step. They get caught up in their everyday work and don't stop to think about the software they're using. Remember, I mentioned that it's human nature to stick with what we know. Our brain loves those repetitive habits because they make us feel comfortable. Making a change is difficult, but it's important to see if an improvement is necessary. Is there better software that could do the job more efficiently and quickly? Does it have more features that you need? Those are the questions you need to ask yourself as you research.

Evaluating Software Updates/Maintenance

When looking for new software, it's important to research and ensure you're getting it from a reputable source. Take the time to evaluate the software and check in on the type of support the company provides. You'll also want to ensure that the software will be regularly updated—look for companies that do their maintenance at night during the work week or on weekends, so you're not stuck trying to update it in the middle of your workday or while you're working with a client.

CHAPTER 9

Microsoft or Google?

You're likely to start a heated debate when you ask people whether Google or Microsoft is better. Spoiler alert: there is no definitive answer. Each product has diehard fans, and each has its strengths and weaknesses. As someone who uses an Apple computer, I tend to lean toward Google. I love the innovation and the ability to collaborate on a Google sheet. Let's dive into which is best and why.

Pros and Cons of Each

I've been using Excel since 2003 as a powerful tool. I use Microsoft and Google products equally, although I tend to prefer PowerPoint over Google Slides just because it has more features. I'm also more comfortable with PowerPoint because I've used it for many years.

Microsoft Teams is a great collaborative tool for my staff and global team. Slack was free and fabulous, even better than Teams, but now they charge to save the data over 90 days. That can get very expensive per user in Slack. We still use Slack as a collaborative tool, but I've been leaning more toward using Team's integration because creating Teams' channels is less expensive.

The debate over whether Excel or Google Sheets is better is a big one. As accountants, we love our spreadsheets. Google Sheets is easy to use and has the check box feature, which I love. However, I have to say that Excel is more robust.

Now, when it comes to Microsoft Excel's ability to have a collaborative place to work on a spreadsheet with a client, Google Sheets is a much better collaborative tool. Excel via Microsoft Office 365's collaboration is a bit wonky and sticky.

Many attorneys use Excel and the Office 365 suite of tools because it works well within a firm.

So which do we think is better? Honestly, it's an individual decision, and you can be like us and use both. Especially since the Google platform is free, you should be paying for Google Suite to get the paid version of Google with the security protocol. Both have pros and cons, but we think using both together is the best way to go.

Best and Worst Products of Each

It's tough to say which product is better or worse for each individual because it depends on what the person is looking for in a spreadsheet program. I will say that if you need something with complex formulas, Microsoft Excel is probably your best bet. The features are powerful and robust. However, I find that most people don't need all those bells and whistles—they only need something for simple arithmetic like adding, subtracting, multiplying, and dividing. Google Sheets allows users to make tables and filters, which people usually need for general office work.

We often use Google Sheets to help us work collaboratively with new clients when onboarding them. For example, when we need to upgrade their chart of accounts, we can show the original on one tab, the suggested chart of accounts on the second tab, and then a collaborative version on the third tab where we meld the two together. This way, we can get our client's approval before importing the new accounts into their file.

Google Docs and Microsoft Word are excellent document processors that provide the basic, simple tools you need daily. They're easy to use with great collaborative features—it's easy to work on a document with someone else regardless of which program you're using. If your firm uses Microsoft Office 365, you can still use Google Docs to collaborate easily with people from outside your organization. However, many of the features unique to Google Docs (such as commenting) can be done in other software programs, so I would say that Google still wins in this category.

Regarding presentations, Google slides are more collaborative; however, if you're creating a slide deck for yourself, PowerPoint has a stronger feature set. I guess it all comes down to who is doing the work and how it's being performed. If you share and collaborate on a document, you'll probably be happier with Google because there will be less friction.

One of the things that I feel is still a weakness of Google's Suite of products is the ability to find a document in your Google Drive after you create it. The search function seems to need fixing in both Google and Microsoft.

Inside Tips for Getting the Best Performance

For optimal performance, it's best to leave the setup of your Microsoft Office 365 to a professional. Trying to do this on your own can often be more trouble than it's worth and can lead to frustration trying to use the software. You always want to keep security in mind when using any online software.

Google, on the other hand, is very easy to use. It's easy to navigate and find what you're looking for. When searching for documents, you'll find that narrowing your search by selecting the document type you are searching for and using the shared drives will set you up for success.

The Google Drive system is unique because you can create a "shared drive" with anyone who uses Google office suite products. When searching for a document, you can "star" it for easy access later or color code your folders to make things more organized. We created a system that when we share a folder in our drive with a client, we make the folder red for "shared with client" files.

For searchability, you can now filter by the type of document. Although the search function has improved, I still need help to look for things I've created and saved. Staying organized is always key.

Suitability as Legal Workflow Software

A law firm's technology needs can't be evaluated with a quick glance—it takes a systematic and comprehensive approach to ensure that the technology being implemented will meet the firm's current and future needs. This process involves taking a look at the firm's workflows, understanding how they use technology currently, and projecting how those needs might change in the future. It also requires evaluating the different options available and choosing the technology that will best fit the firm's needs.

Evaluating Your Law Firm Needs

As trusted advisors, our clients often ask us which product or platform they should use for their law firm. Google or Microsoft—the (new) age-old question. Because we work with many law firms, our clients know we have a lot of experience to draw from. And while we tend to lean on Google products because we use all Apple computers, we also have experience with Office 365 and have invested in that product so that we can work fluidly and complementary with our clients. I do see more firms moving toward using the Microsoft Office 365 suite of products. And, most law firms tend to use PCs over Apple computers.

Ultimately, it comes down to what you're most comfortable with and what makes the most sense for you. My best advice is to invest in the software by paying for a subscription. Paying for the software guarantees you'll use the latest and most secure features that are often updated.

I remember being so excited when I first got Dropbox and LogMeIn for free. I loved that I no longer had to go to client offices. I set up one Dropbox account for my personal tax returns and one for my business. I used it to collaborate with clients, and then one day, a client told me they could see everything in my personal folder under a separate account. Somehow, I'd linked the two accounts to my one username.

Paying for software may seem unnecessary, but it's an important investment. I learned this the hard way when a client could access my personal tax return through the free software I was using. Because the software was free, I had no legal recourse or way to prevent the client from seeing my sensitive information. It was a hard lesson to learn, but I'm glad it happened with my own data instead of a client's. I know free software is not worth the risk when protecting my clients' confidential information.

Evaluating Microsoft/Google Support

Regarding customer support, both Google and Microsoft excel in this area—especially Microsoft. They will follow up with you to ensure that any problems you're experiencing have been resolved to your satisfaction. When you call them, you will always be talking to a dedicated support representative who will go above and beyond to help you solve your issue.

Google's customer support is also very good, although you may only sometimes be talking to a live person. However, a chat option is available, and they will follow up with you after the chat to ensure that your problem has been resolved. The best option for you might depend on whether you want to talk to a live person or chat.

CHAPTER 10

The Future

Legal Accounting and Blockchain

The future of legal technology is likely to involve a wide range of innovative technologies including blockchain.

Blockchain is a decentralized, distributed ledger technology that allows transactions to be recorded and verified securely without a central authority. It has the potential to revolutionize many industries, including the legal industry.

Why Blockchain?

There are several potential benefits of using blockchain in the legal industry, including:

- Blockchain technology creates tamper-proof records, which can be useful for legal documents and agreements that need to be stored long term. This increased security can give you peace of mind knowing that your records are safe and sound.
- Blockchain technology can help to improve transparency around transactions, making it easier to track and manage intellectual property ownership such as patents and trademarks. By creating a transparent and verifiable record of transactions, blockchain could help to streamline the management of intellectual property (IP) rights and reduce the risk of fraud or error.

  This could be a valuable tool for businesses and individuals who need to keep track of their IP rights, and it could help to make the process of managing these rights more efficient and secure.
- Blockchain can automate and streamline various legal processes, such as dispute resolution and contract execution, which could save time and reduce costs. This would allow for a more efficient legal system overall.
- There are many ways in which blockchain could help increase efficiency within the legal industry. Automating certain processes and creating secure, tamper-proof records are just two examples of how blockchain technology can be used to streamline the work of lawyers and other legal professionals.

Blockchain technology has the potential to improve security, transparency, and efficiency in the legal industry, which could lead to cost savings and increased effectiveness.

Legal Applications for Blockchain

Smart Contracts

Smart contracts can offer several benefits for lawyers, including the following.

Increased efficiency: Smart contracts can automate many of the tasks involved in the legal process, such as the execution of contracts and the tracking of compliance requirements. This can reduce the time and effort required to complete these tasks, freeing up lawyers to focus on higher value work.

Reduced risk of errors: Smart contracts can eliminate the risk of errors caused by manual data entry or misunderstandings of contract terms. Because they are executed automatically based on predefined rules, smart contracts can help ensure that agreements are carried out as intended.

Improved transparency: Smart contracts can provide a clear and auditable record of the terms of an agreement and the actions taken under it. This can help lawyers to better understand the legal implications of their actions and can make it easier to resolve disputes if they arise.

Enhanced security: Smart contracts can be stored and executed on a blockchain, which provides a secure and immutable record of their execution. This can help to reduce the risk of fraud or tampering and can give lawyers greater confidence in the integrity of their agreements.

Overall, smart contracts have the potential to significantly streamline the legal process and increase the efficiency and accuracy of legal work.

Land Registry

A blockchain-based land registry is a digital system for recording and managing ownership and transfer of real estate. It uses blockchain technology to create a secure, transparent, and tamper-proof record of property ownership and transfer.

There are several legal applications for a blockchain-based land registry, including the following.

Verification of ownership: A blockchain-based land registry can provide an accurate and verifiable record of ownership, making it easier to determine who owns a particular piece of property.

Efficient transfer of ownership: The use of smart contracts on a blockchain-based land registry can automate the process of transferring ownership, reducing the time and effort required to complete the transaction.

Improved security: A blockchain-based land registry can help to reduce the risk of fraud and tampering by providing a secure and immutable record of ownership and transfer.

Increased transparency: A blockchain-based land registry can provide a clear and auditable record of ownership and transfer, making it easier to track the history of a particular piece of property.

Overall, a blockchain-based land registry has the potential to significantly improve the efficiency, accuracy, and security of real estate transactions.

Intellectual Property Rights

Blockchain technology has the potential to revolutionize the way that intellectual property rights are managed and enforced. Some potential legal applications for blockchain in this area include the following.

Registration and protection of intellectual property: A blockchain-based system could be used to register and protect intellectual property, such as trademarks, patents, and copyrights. By creating a secure and immutable record of ownership, a blockchain-based system could help to deter counterfeiting and infringement.

Licensing and royalty payments: A blockchain-based system could be used to track and manage the licensing of intellectual property and the payment of royalties. Smart contracts could be used to automate the process of paying royalties based on the use of the intellectual property.

Enforcement of intellectual property rights: A blockchain-based system could be used to track and enforce intellectual property rights, such as by helping to identify and stop the unauthorized use of protected works.

Overall, the use of blockchain technology in the management and enforcement of intellectual property rights has the potential to improve the efficiency and accuracy of these processes and provide greater protection for intellectual property owners.

Chain of Custody

Chain of custody refers to the documentation and tracking of the movement of evidence or physical items from the time they are seized or collected until they are presented in court. Blockchain technology has the potential to improve the accuracy and security of the chain of custody process in several ways as follows.

Secure and immutable record-keeping: A blockchain-based system can provide a secure and immutable record of the movement and handling of evidence or physical items. This can help to ensure that the chain of custody is not compromised, and that the integrity of the evidence is preserved.

Improved transparency: A blockchain-based system can provide a clear and auditable record of the chain of custody, making it easier to track the movement and handling of evidence or physical items. This can help to reduce the risk of errors or tampering and can provide a more complete record for use in court.

Automation of processes: Smart contracts on a blockchain-based system can automate certain aspects of the chain of custody process, such as the tracking of deadlines and the notification of relevant parties when items are moved or handled.

Overall, the use of blockchain technology in the chain of custody process can help to improve the accuracy, security, and transparency of this process and can help to ensure the integrity of the evidence being presented in court.

Litigation and Settlements

Blockchain technology has the potential to revolutionize the litigation and settlement processes in several ways as follows.

Secure and immutable record-keeping: A blockchain-based system can provide a secure and immutable record of legal documents and other information related to a case. This can help to ensure the integrity of the information and reduce the risk of errors or tampering.

Improved transparency: A blockchain-based system can provide a clear and auditable record of legal proceedings, making it easier for parties to track the progress of a case and understand the legal implications of their actions.

Automation of processes: Smart contracts on a blockchain-based system can automate certain aspects of the litigation process, such as the tracking of deadlines and the notification of relevant parties when certain actions need to be taken.

Enhanced security: A blockchain-based system can help to reduce the risk of cyberattacks and other security breaches, ensuring that sensitive legal information is protected.

Overall, the use of blockchain technology in the litigation process can help to improve the efficiency, accuracy, and security of legal proceedings.

Financial Transactions

Blockchain technology has the potential to revolutionize the financial transaction process in several ways:

- **Secure and immutable record-keeping**: A blockchain-based system can provide a secure and immutable record of financial transactions. This can help to ensure the integrity of the information and reduce the risk of errors or tampering.
- **Improved transparency**: A blockchain-based system can provide a clear and auditable record of financial transactions, making it easier for parties to track the movement of funds and understand the financial implications of their actions.
- **Automation of processes**: Smart contracts on a blockchain-based system can automate certain aspects of the financial transaction process, such as the execution of contracts and the tracking of compliance requirements.

Enhanced security: A blockchain-based system can help to reduce the risk of cyberattacks and other security breaches, ensuring that sensitive financial information is protected.

Possible Future Legal Applications

Automated Settlements of Security Transactions

One possible future legal application of automated settlements of security transactions is the use of smart contracts to automate the process of settling trades. Smart contracts could be programmed to automatically execute the transfer of securities and funds based on predefined rules, such as the completion of certain conditions or the passage of a certain amount of time.

This could significantly streamline the settlement process, reducing the time and effort required to complete trades and reducing the risk of errors or delays. It could also help to improve the efficiency and transparency of the settlement process, as all parties would have a clear and auditable record of the terms of the trade and the actions taken to settle it.

Another potential legal application of automated settlements is the use of smart contracts to enforce compliance with regulatory requirements. For example, smart contracts could be programmed to automatically check for compliance with know-your-customer (KYC) and anti money laundering (AML) rules before executing a trade.

Overall, automated settlements using smart contracts have the potential to significantly improve the efficiency, accuracy, and security of the settlement process for security transactions.

Using Digital Assets to Complete Payments

One possible future legal application of using digital assets to complete payments is the use of cryptocurrency to facilitate cross-border transactions. Because cryptocurrencies are decentralized and can be easily transferred across national borders, they have the potential to significantly improve the efficiency of international payments.

Another potential legal application of digital assets is the use of smart contracts to automate the payment process. Smart contracts could be programmed to automatically execute payments based on predefined conditions, such as the completion of a task or the passage of a certain amount of time. This could significantly streamline the payment process, reducing the time and effort required to complete transactions and reducing the risk of errors or delays.

Another potential legal application of digital assets is the use of non-fungible tokens (NFTs) to represent ownership of unique assets, such as art, collectibles, or real estate. NFTs could be used to track the ownership and transfer of these assets securely and transparently, providing a clear and auditable record of ownership.

Overall, the use of digital assets to complete payments has the potential to significantly improve the efficiency, accuracy, and security of financial transactions.

Digital Wallet Instead of Escrow Accounts

A digital wallet is a digital platform that allows users to store, manage, and transfer digital assets, such as cryptocurrency. In some cases, a digital wallet could potentially be used instead of an escrow account to hold funds or assets during a transaction.

One advantage of using a digital wallet instead of an escrow account is that it can provide a more secure and transparent record of the transaction. Because digital wallets are typically built on blockchain technology, they can provide a secure and immutable record of the funds or assets being held. This can help to reduce the risk of fraud or tampering and can provide a clear and auditable record of the transaction.

Another advantage of using a digital wallet is that it can facilitate the automatic execution of transactions based on predefined conditions. For example, a smart contract could be programmed to automatically release funds from the digital wallet to the appropriate parties once certain conditions are met, such as the completion of a task or the passage of a certain amount of time. This can significantly streamline the transaction process and reduce the risk of errors or delays.

Overall, the use of a digital wallet instead of an escrow account has the potential to improve the efficiency, accuracy, and security of transactions. However, it is important to carefully consider the risks and benefits of using a digital wallet in place of an escrow account, as well as any legal or regulatory considerations.

CHAPTER 11

Summary and Final Comments

My Recommendations for a Modern Law Firm

Evaluate Your Firm's Specific Needs

When it comes to becoming a modern law firm, you need to look at the firm's needs overall. If you're just beginning, you will want to ensure you have good basic hardware and equipment. You will probably want a legal billing or a good legal practice management system, a good scanner, and office processing software, whether it is Microsoft 365, or you use Google Suite.

If you are a mid-sized firm, you'll probably have a receptionist in place. If your firm isn't large enough to support that, you may want to hire or outsource a virtual receptionist.

Any successful law practice will need a good system to track its leads to see if they eventually become clients and follow how successful the client relationship is from that first touchpoint. A good CRM system will be important for the law firm's profitability.

Being a cloud-based firm and not having any paper around might seem unusual for a law firm, but it means you're more proactive. Having a system in place for all the documents is as important as having the paper in the files. By making use of cloud storage, you can be more organized and responsive to your client's needs without having to worry about losing important paperwork.

Making the switch to a paperless office doesn't have to be daunting. Once you do it, you'll likely wonder why you didn't do it sooner! Not only will it save you time and money in the long run but having everything stored electronically will make your life easier if there is ever an audit.

Paperless offices are more secure than their paper counterparts if you have the right system in place. If you're worried about going paperless, research and find a system that will work for you and your team. I promise you won't regret it!

When it comes to optimizing your office's workflow, planning is key. Document each office task and determine what software can be used to automate your processes. Many legal technology tools can help you streamline your workflow and free up time for other tasks.

Size

I have worked with many attorneys who need help connecting their software to QuickBooks. They are missing out on a valuable part of the software! Even solo or solo +1 attorneys may find that they can automate many of their processes and use a virtual staff. I am seeing this more and more with completely remote law practices.

Securing your data is a critical step that must be addressed. The ABA mandates that you protect your client's data. The data must be protected and confidential for physical paperwork and electronic documents.

Scope

If you want to work smarter, not harder, you need to start by looking at your current systems and processes. See where potential improvements can be made, then put new software and documentation in place to streamline things. Once you thoroughly understand the tasks that need to be done, you can best match employee skills and talents to those jobs. Then everyone in the company will know exactly what they need to do and how it should be done.

We worked with a firm using software that needed to be designed specifically for their practice area. This was a mid-market-sized firm with many attorneys and working parts. Nobody had looked at the strategy of why this software was being used, and we found in the end that every-body needed to be using it in the right way. What was supposed to be protecting the firm from overpaying clients when matters were settled successfully, meant someone taking a ton of time to see the details and ensure everything was noticed.

This person manually created and tracked all company expenses on spreadsheets, creating confusion and mystery among other employees. This is not an effective or efficient way to work. When one person is solely responsible for such an important task, it not only gives them a false sense of security but also puts the company at risk if that person is ever unable to do their job. A system everyone can understand, and follow is crucial for any business.

Do you want your firm to be tech-forward with a team that knows the entire picture of the systems in place?

Pain Points (Identify Recurring Problems)

Now, I'm not here to tell you that software can solve every problem at a law firm. However, it's important to identify any pain points and anything that continually happens at your firm, causing delays in processing and getting the funds in the door. It's important to make sure that your clients are happy and that these clients are being attended to and cared for. Happy clients' equal referrals. It's simple.

But manual processes can hold you back. If you're at a point where you want your firm to grow, but you can't see the light at the end of the tunnel, it's time to hire somebody who knows how to get you there. How can you manage these workflows and make them smoother so that you can expand your services? You will have questions, but some of the answers will not be in your area of expertise or comfort zone. Hiring an expert will serve you well.

The solution to all your problems will not always be that shiny object of brand-new software, but there's a lot of law firm tech out there that will help your firm do things you may still be doing the old-fashioned way.

IT or Tech Staff

Depending on the size of the firm, you may have an IT team in place, or you may have someone on staff or retainer to handle all the connectivity of the office staff and how they access the company files. It's important to ensure that all software processes work with one another and can be handled very simply by users.

With most firms, that IT person can be a blessing or an annoyance because some things are not working, and it takes a while to get the system set up. The right IT firm will smartly and securely help your firm work. Security is at the utmost, even if your firm is mostly remote.

Identify How Much Outside Support You Will Need

The smaller firms, by design, will need to hire that IT person who works remotely as the outsourced specialist to help run a cohesive office with the best technology. It is important to set up the system upfront and properly, especially if your firm has many people who work remotely. It's important to find the right IT specialist who understands the technology you selected and why it's right for your firm, is familiar with the legal industry, and is available when you need them. Any downtime in your workflow is costly.

Who Will Provide Ongoing Training for Staff and Employees?

Training staff on new software is more difficult when they are all in multiple offices. It is also critical to have ongoing training as you select software that continues to improve. It is far too easy to use the legal tech "just enough" and not continue to use the new features as they are added. Think of yourself when you get a new "upgraded" phone—you learn how to do just enough to continue your habitual uses and ignore many of the newer features. You are paying for the full package; don't waste your money on helpful features that no one understands enough to use.

Often, the software comes with training where the software vendor trains you, and some include certifications that must be retaken annually to stay certified.

Budgeting for Software Maintenance, Training, and Unexpected Issues

One challenge in budgeting for legal tech is that it can take some time to determine the annual cost. You must do a program inventory (refer to the inventory sheets in Chapter 6) to see what software is used and the actual cost to the firm. Look at your users to see who is listed as a user (are they still with the firm?) and see what other firms in your practice area are using. Maybe it is time to change, but remember, with change comes a disruption in the workflow and training time. It doesn't always make sense to change just because there's something newer available.

A law firm's technology needs can't be evaluated with a quick glance—it takes a systematic and comprehensive approach to ensure that the technology being implemented will meet the firm's current and future needs. This process involves looking at the firm's workflows, understanding how they use technology currently, and projecting how those needs might change in the future. It also requires evaluating the different options available and choosing the technology that will best fit the firm's needs.

1. Identify the firm's business goals and objectives: It is important to understand the firm's goals and objectives to determine which technology will be most helpful in achieving them.

2. Start by conducting a technology audit: This involves reviewing the law firm's current technology infrastructure, including hardware, software, and networks, to identify strengths and weaknesses.

3. Assess the firm's current and future technology needs: This may involve considering factors such as size, growth plans, and practice areas.

4. Determine the firm's budget for technology: This will help narrow down the options and ensure that the firm can afford the technology it needs.

5. Research and compare technology options: This may involve looking at different software and hardware options and evaluating their features and pricing.

6. Seek input from employees: It is important to get input on their technology needs and preferences, as they will be using the technology daily.

7. Develop a technology plan: Once the firm's technology needs have been identified, a plan should be developed to implement and manage the technology, including budgeting for ongoing maintenance and updates.

By following these steps, a law firm can effectively evaluate its specific technology needs and develop a plan to implement the necessary technology to support its business goals and objectives.

Establish a Centralized Software Platform

I often refer to QuickBooks as the center of the universe; it is when you look at the power behind the software that helps you make smart decisions on the trajectory of your firm. The ways you can extract data, whether you use spreadsheet sync, Fathom, Reach Reporting, Live Plan, or any other currently existing software, you will find you have a lot of metrics at your fingertips. Layering on LeanLaw, Clio, MyCase or any other legal software just sweetens the pot and makes QuickBooks work like a program designed for a law firm.

Regularly Evaluate Practice Efficiency

Practice efficiency can be determined by checking in with the staff and "job shadowing" them to see how they follow office protocol and complete the work. Are they reverting to spreadsheets? Or are they using the chosen software to its fullest capability? Good software evolves and grows. Many have a monthly newsletter or webinars to broadcast the new features and what is on the roadmap. Those few minutes or hours on a webinar may be invaluable in time savings down the road. Consider assigning staff to review that information regularly.

Check for Outdated Software

Outdated software can slow you down and can cost the firm money. As the business owner, you may need to know that the software is crashing, not connected to the accounting, or even validated and reconciled. Just like the annual software inventory, it is critical to research what you are using and what version you are using. Consider developing a process for reporting all such events as crashing and outages to a central source for compilation and evaluation.

Review Data Security

What Are Your Firm's Vulnerabilities?

It is very easy to just pass this step by and disregard it. That is until a breach occurs, and your whole firm comes to a grinding halt. Even worse, if there is a ransomware attack, you may have to pay a bounty to get the data released. And there is a strong possibility that you pay, and they don't release the software. Take the time to educate and reeducate the staff on possible ways the bad guys can infiltrate a firm.

Establish More Secure Procedures

Two-factor verification: Implement two factors whenever it is offered. Those few seconds a day will save you from hours or days of heartache and headache.

    Periodically advise staff on avoiding phishing scams, and so on: This training area won't cut the mustard if done only annually. This step should be taken once each quarter minimally. You can even designate a staff member to stay on top of the current threat and notify the staff to keep them updated.

Periodically advise staff on password security tips: If you have yet to review staff passwords, this one tends to be one of the most eye-opening steps. You can do a simple review with staff to update the master list of what software each person uses, what user permissions are in place, and what the password is to access the data.

Regularly update staff about new or emerging cyber threats: This can be done as easily as sending out a newsletter from the top software protection companies. But you need to review it with staff to ensure you know they are reading the newsletter. People get busy doing their work, but knowledge is power.

Consider Annual Tech or IT Security Audit

Outside eyes on your security protocol are the best money spent. We all think we can do every task in our business, but this one should be addressed. These firms are trained to look at what you have in place, check in with staff, and review the needs of your law firm. Additionally, this may be a requirement of your Cyber insurance provider, or you can get a discount on your insurance when you hire that expert to review security.

Final Comments

Law firms are increasingly looking to technology to help achieve goals such as increasing efficiency, improving the client experience, and producing better firm financials. By prioritizing the benefits of technology investments, firms can realize these gains while reducing costs.

With the high-powered boost that AI-driven data analytics could give a firm, it's clear that AI is here and will be part of our future! As an impending software purchase, AI-powered legal research is something to watch. This is especially true for litigation support with AI and natural language processing. These are the top choices for new tech solution purchases that show that law firm business leaders are not shying away from advanced technology.

Legal technology can give law firms a competitive edge in the marketplace. Many business leaders in the legal industry have realized this and are working to catch up and implement the latest technologies. Firms that wait to do so may find themselves at a disadvantage.

All-in-all, following the steps outlined in this book should put you in a great place to be that modern law firm. Legal tech does evolve, and while for today I recommend LeanLaw and Clio, tomorrow it may look different. Hiring an expert who knows your industry and can provide you with the foundation of your legal accounting ecosphere and other tools that help set you up for a smooth, automated future is just the beginning.

Security should not be an afterthought! In today's world of remote workers, it is ultraimportant that you have your security in place—right down to the remote worker's computer. You must control who has access and when it is used.

As you can see, it all comes down to workflows and processes. Those two items will allow your firm to run smoothly and efficiently. And best of all, profitably!

About the Author

Lynda Artesani is an esteemed legal accountant and a data migration specialist. She is committed to helping law firms embrace a future characterized by efficiency, innovation, and adaptability. She is a cofounder at The Proper Trust, LLC, an accounting firm that specializes in working with attorneys, and she utilizes her vast expertise to simplify legal accounting processes and modernize operations.

> *It's essential for law firms to adapt and stay ahead of the game. With the rapid advancement of technology and the changing expectations of clients, modernizing your law firm is no longer a choice—it's a necessity.*

—Lynda Artesani
Founder/Co-founder
Artesani Accounting
The Proper Trust, LLC
The Accountant's Law Lab

The Accountant's Law Lab is a coaching platform with courses, a mastermind, and one-on-one sessions to teach bookkeepers or legal assistants, and paralegals legal accounting.

Index

Personal computers (PCs) to legal
industry
accounts payable, 7–8
analyzing briefs, 4–5
attorney productivity, 11–12
bookkeeping/accounting, 5
business KPIs, 11
client contact, 8–9
data base concept, 9
legal research, 3–4
marketing services, 10–11
processing/analyzing client
information, 9
profitable clients/cases/areas, 12
scheduling/tracking billable hours,
9–10
tracking accounts receivable, 5–7
Post-COVID adjustments
client contact, 80–82
office *vs.* remote, 77–80

QuickBooks Desktop, 6, 40

Risk, outdated software
AI processors, 39
big data, 39
cloud solutions, 40
computer chip cost, 39
crashing computers, 37
cyberattacks, 41
decreased productivity and lost
time, 38
FEMA, 44
internet users, 39
LeanLaw, 40
metrics, 38
mobile devices, 44
ransomware, 41–44
security threat, 44–45
smartphone usage, 40
software vulnerabilities, 40–41
vulnerability, 38

Staff training
handling questions, 87–88
in-person/online videos, 87
regular follow-ups, 87–88

remote staff training, 87
training effectiveness evaluation,
88–89

Technology introduction
change in tech steps, 85
cloud-based software, 84–85
dos and don'ts, 83–84
manager buy-in and support, 89
outside assistance, 86
product effectiveness, 89–91
staff training, 87–89
vendor staff training programs,
85–86
Tech Stack identification
Clio, 70–71
Cosmolex, 70
evaluation worksheet, 69
inventory worksheet, 69
Lawcus, 70
LeanLaw, 70
legal workflow software, 72–75
medium to large law firms, 76
MyCase, 71
Practice Panther, 70
reconciliation process, 70
small law firms, 75–76

Virtual law firm
challenges, 66
confidentiality, 66
employees' productivity, 65–66
equity partners, 64
ethical questions, 65
FEIN number and licenses, 64
fraud, 66
tools, 67
trends, 63–64
wellness, 66
Vulnerability to hackers
AI and blockchain, 48
cyberterrorism, 48–49
e-mailing sensitive data, 48
lack of vendor support, 49–50
malware attacks, 46
phishing e-mails, 47
ransom payment, 46

OTHER TITLES IN THE BUSINESS LAW AND CORPORATE RISK MANAGEMENT COLLECTION

- *Mobilizing the C-Suite* by Frank Riccardi
- *Enhanced Enterprise Risk Management* by John Sidwell and Peter Hlavnicka
- *A Corporate Librarian's Guide to Information Governance and Data Privacy* by Phyllis L. Elin
- *A Government Librarian's Guide to Information Governance and Data Privacy* by Phyllis Elin and Max Rapaport
- *Protecting the Brand, Volume II* by Peter Hlavnicka and Anthony M. Keats
- *Can. Trust. Will.* by Leeza Garber and Scott Olson
- *Protecting the Brand, Volume I* by Peter Hlavnicka and Anthony M. Keats
- *Business Sustainability* by Zabihollah Rezaee
- *Business Sustainability Factors of Performance, Risk, and Disclosure* by Zabihollah Rezaee
- *The Gig Mafia* by David M. Shapiro
- *Guerrilla Warfare in the Corporate Jungle* by K. F. Dochartaigh
- *Consumer Protection in E-Retailing in ASEAN* by Huong Ha
- *A Book About Blockchain* by Rajat Rajbhandari
- *Successful Cybersecurity Professionals* by Steven Brown

Concise and Applied Business Books

The Collection listed above is one of 30 business subject collections that Business Expert Press has grown to make BEP a premiere publisher of print and digital books. Our concise and applied books are for…

- Professionals and Practitioners
- Faculty who adopt our books for courses
- Librarians who know that BEP's Digital Libraries are a unique way to offer students ebooks to download, not restricted with any digital rights management
- Executive Training Course Leaders
- Business Seminar Organizers

Business Expert Press books are for anyone who needs to dig deeper on business ideas, goals, and solutions to everyday problems. Whether one print book, one ebook, or buying a digital library of 110 ebooks, we remain the affordable and smart way to be business smart. For more information, please visit www.businessexpertpress.com, or contact sales@businessexpertpress.com.